ENGLAND'S LAST MEDIEVAL MONASTERY

SYON ABBEY 1415–2015

England's Last Medieval Monastery

Syon Abbey
1415–2015

E. A. Jones

GRACEWING

First published in England in 2015

by

Gracewing
2 Southern Avenue
Leominster
Herefordshire HR6 0QF
United Kingdom

www.gracewing.co.uk

ISBN 978 085244 872 4

Typeset by Word and Page, Chester

Cover design by Bernardita Peña Hurtado

CONTENTS

FOREWORD

by Sr Anne Smyth, abbess of Syon 1976–2011

The closure of Syon Abbey, South Brent, on 7 September 2011, took place exactly 67 years from the day when Sr M. Julie Holland, one of the three remaining sisters, entered as a postulant. Such a coincidence of dates marked much of Syon's history. One celebration was certainly planned. The installation of Mother M. Teresa Jocelyn as perpetual abbess on 21 April 1921 commemorated the elections of the first abbess and Confessor General of Syon on 21 April 1421, five hundred years previously. The dates 1421 and 1921 were engraved on the new abbatial pectoral cross given to the abbess on that day. Just a few years later the first mass at South Brent, the day after the move from Chudleigh, on 11 November 1925, coincided with the date in 1431 when the community was re-enclosed after the move from Twickenham to the new abbey at Isleworth. But the one anniversary which the community always faithfully observed was the death of our royal founder, King Henry V. On 31 August each year we remembered his passing with the celebration of a requiem mass and the Office of the Dead, a commitment which continues up to the present time, as he had requested in the foundation charter.

From the fifteenth-century records available in the British Library, the copy of the Wanderings of Syon written in Lisbon, through to the less formal 'Syon Notes' which can be found in copies of The Poor Souls' Friend and St Joseph's Monitor from the late nineteenth century to the 1960s, and the meticulous recording of the obituaries of the sisters, brothers and major benefactors over the centuries, the community was conscious, not only of its history but the need to remember with joy and thanksgiving those who had preceded us. In recalling those who had suffered for their faith, such as the martyr St Richard Reynolds, Br Thomas Brownell, who had died in prison, or Sr Elizabeth Sander, who spent six years in Winchester in prison; or the fire in Lisbon which destroyed so much, and a hundred years later the earthquake in that city, quite apart from the stories of hunger and other dangers suffered following the second exile from the community's homeland, no sister could fail to be moved by such heroism. We were challenged to follow in their footsteps and live our rule as fully as possible and to the best of our ability.

The unifying elements of this history of the community are two-fold: the Rule of our Saviour, as revealed to St Bridget in 1346, and the Bridgettine Breviary, as used by the sisters, although not continuously from the time they were in Lisbon until after the return to England in 1861, but never forgotten and taken up again with renewed fervour in the early twentieth century.

In order to tell this 'story' to a new readership I have great joy in welcoming Professor Jones's book. I hope it will encourage many to enquire further into the lives of our brothers and sisters through these last six centuries. May their witness and faithfulness to their religious life, their constant hope of returning to England during the periods of exile and their prayer for their homeland be an inspiration to many.

PREFACE

In 2015 we celebrate the six hundredth anniversary of the founding of Syon Abbey, England's only house of the Bridgettine order, one of the last great foundations of medieval England, and the only English monastic community able to trace its history in an unbroken line from the Middle Ages to the present day. It is a long and winding story, that begins by the Thames in Middlesex, crosses the Spanish Netherlands and northern France, and spends two and a half centuries in Lisbon, before it ends up in south-west England. There is drama on the way – persecution and martyrdom under Henry VIII, brushes with English mercenaries and Calvinist mobs, pirates, wars, fire and earthquake – but sustaining the community throughout is a strong sense of English identity and an unshakeable faith.

This short account is designed for anyone interested in Syon's story. It attempts to summarise the present state of our knowledge of the abbey and its history, and is based on a large body of scholarly work, some of which is listed in the Suggestions for Further Reading at the end of the book. My debts to the authors and works mentioned there will be obvious. It has become obvious to me, also, how uneven has been the work on the community's history to date: it feels as if we understand quite a lot about certain periods (most notably the Middle Ages), whilst others (the years in Lisbon, or the twentieth century) still present many opportunities for further research. If others follow, and prove almost everything I have said in these chapters to have been inaccurate or insufficiently detailed, I will be happy.

A brief note on names and quotations. Until *c.* 1900 nuns of Syon were known by their own names. Around that time, they adopted the practice of taking a 'name in religion' on their profession, thereafter going by a saint's name (often a male saint). All nuns prefaced this name with the name of Mary, to whom the Bridgettine order has a special devotion. I have abbreviated this, but added the surname whenever possible or relevant (thus, for instance, the mid-twentieth-century Abbess M. Magdalen Nevin). Quotations from primary texts are given in modernised spellings, and I have sometimes adjusted punctuation and capitalisation to make them read more easily for modern readers. Translations of Latin and other languages are my own unless stated otherwise.

I have too many debts to acknowledge them all here. Colleagues who have written the works listed in the Suggestions for Further Reading, and whom I have pestered repeatedly, know who they are. Special thanks are due to Jonathan Nicholson at Marley House. I am grateful to the staff of the libraries where I have worked, and to the institutions and individuals who have given permission for me to use their material for illustrations. Particular thanks here to Harold Deakin of Northallerton for his wonderful portraits of the nuns taken at Marley House in the early 1980s. For all their help with the Syon Abbey archive, I am most grateful to Christine Faunch and the staff of Special Collections in the University of Exeter Library, amongst whom I should make special mention of Gemma Poulton, for her photographs, and Angela Mandrioli, who has borne the brunt of my many requests for material.

Above all, though, I want to thank Sr Anne Smyth. Sr Anne has spoken tirelessly to me of Syon's history, and read patiently and attentively what I have made of it, alerted me to new lines of enquiry and saved me from some egregious errors, shared materials and lent photographs. It is impossible to come away from a meeting with her without renewed enthusiasm for Syon and its history. Without her, her sisters and their predecessors, there would have been no story to tell.

OUTLINE CHRONOLOGY

1391 Canonisation of St Bridget of Sweden.
1406 Henry Lord FitzHugh at Vadstena announces intention to found a Bridgettine monastery.
1415 Foundation of Syon Abbey at Twickenham by Henry V.
1420 First professions at Syon.
1431 Community moves to new site in Isleworth and is re-enclosed.
1481 Thomas Betson resigns as rector of Wimbish prior to entering Syon to become the brothers' librarian.
1488 Consecration of abbey church.
1500 Betson's *Profitable treatise* printed by Wynkyn de Worde.
1533 Syon named in the trial of Elizabeth Barton, the 'Holy Maid of Kent'.
1535 Execution of Syon brother, Richard Reynolds.
1539 Expulsion of community and granting of pensions.
1557 Syon returns to England under Queen Mary.
1559 Death of Mary; community begins its exile in the Low Countries.
1576 Death of Abbess Katherine Palmer.
1580 Following sack of Mechelen, community leaves Spanish Netherlands for Rouen.
1584 Profession of Seth Foster, and his election as confessor general.
1594 Henri IV becomes king of France; Syon community leaves for Lisbon.
1599 Community established in its own premises in Mocambo, Lisbon.
1640 Portugal declares independence from Spain.
1651 Convent destroyed by fire.
1695 Death of George Griffin, the last brother of Syon.
1755 Lisbon earthquake.
1791 Roman Catholic Relief Act permits Catholic worship in England.
1809 Failed attempt at return to England under Abbess Dorothy Halford.
1840 Publication of Aungier's *History and Antiquities of Syon Monastery*.
1861 Return of Syon Abbey to England, initially at Spetisbury (Dorset).

1886   Beatification of Richard Reynolds.

1887   Community moves to Chudleigh.

1925   Community moves to Marley House, South Brent.

1970   Canonisation of Richard Reynolds.

1990   Community moves to specially designed accommodation in converted stables of Marley House.

2011   Syon Abbey closes.

2015   Celebrations for sexcentenary of Syon Abbey's foundation.

✛ Prologue ✛

IT IS 6 AUGUST 2011, the Feast of the Transfiguration. In a small, modern chapel in south Devon, mass is being celebrated by the bishop of Plymouth, the right reverend Christopher Budd, assisted by a group of monks from the nearby Buckfast Abbey. The congregation of some twenty friends and well-wishers fills one side of the chapel. Down the centre of the room is a wooden screen painted with seven life-size male figures, representing the five protomartyrs of the English reformation, and SS Thomas More and John Fisher, who suffered soon after they did. On the other side of the partition is a small group of elderly nuns: the three remaining sisters of England's only house of the Order of the Most Holy Saviour, or Bridgettines, and the only English monastery able to trace its history in an unbroken line from the Middle Ages until the present day. We are there to celebrate the community's one hundred and fifty years in the diocese of Plymouth, and the anniversary of their return to England – at the end of three centuries of exile in the Netherlands, France and Portugal – in 1861. But all of us know that, with the sale of the convent buildings agreed and arrangements for the removal in place, we are also marking the closure of Syon Abbey, and the final chapter in the community's six-hundred-year history.

I

⊹ *Beginnings* ⊹

THEIR STORY BEGINS IN 1406, in Sweden, with a royal wedding. A marriage between Philippa, daughter of Henry IV of England, and Erik of Pomerania, king of the Kalmar union of Scandinavian nations, Sweden, Norway and Denmark, had been negotiated back in 1401, when Henry, in the years immediately following his seizure of the throne from Richard II, was eager to establish his line among the legitimate ruling dynasties of Europe. In 1406 Philippa reached the age of twelve, the legal age for marriage in the Middle Ages (Erik was twice that age), and set sail for Sweden. Accompanying her was Henry FitzHugh, lord of Ravensworth in Yorkshire, and a close ally of the king. The marriage was celebrated at Lund Cathedral on 26 October. At the conclusion of the festivities, the party set off for Stockholm but broke their journey to visit the abbey of Vadstena.

Vadstena was the mother house of the Order of the Most Holy Saviour, founded by St Bridget of Sweden in the fourteenth century. It was a groundbreaking order founded by a new kind of saint. Bridget, who was proclaimed a patron saint of Europe by Pope John Paul II in 1999, was (in contrast to the other women saints celebrated in the Middle Ages) neither a nun nor a virgin martyr. Born into a noble Swedish family in 1303, she was married at age 14 to Ulf Gudmarsson, law-man (regional governor) of Närke in south-central Sweden, to whom she bore eight children. Bridget and Ulf were also intensely religious, and when Bridget reached her late thirties they decided to commit themselves to lives of devout chastity. In the event, Ulf died soon afterwards, in 1344, and shortly after that Bridget (who had had visions since childhood) received the first of many revelations on a range of topics, from devotional visions of Christ's nativity and passion to political prophecies concerning the Hundred Years War and the Great Schism. In 1346, on a visit to what was then a royal palace at Vadstena,

St Bridget giving her rule to her order. Woodblock print, Augsburg, *c.* 1480–1500.
© Trustees of the British Museum.

she received a revelation in which Christ appeared and instructed her to found a new religious order, the Order of the Most Holy Saviour.

Houses of the order were to be for both men and women, though in Bridget's vision the women took precedence over the men. The composition and design of the monastic community and buildings were specified precisely in the revelation. A fully populated Bridgettine monastery would have eighty-five members: sixty nuns, thirteen priest-brothers, four deacons, and eight laybrothers. The numbers were symbolic: the thirteen priests stood for the twelve apostles plus Paul; the deacons (who were expected to take on a clerical role) recalled the four great doctors of the Church (saints Augustine, Jerome, Ambrose and Gregory), while the total of eighty-five made reference to the thirteen apostles plus seventy-two disciples commissioned by Christ in Luke 10. Spiritual direction for the monastery would be the responsibility of one of the priests, the confessor general, but final authority in all matters belonged to the abbess. The men and women would live in separate courts within the monastery, coming together only for worship in the abbey church. Even here, strict separation would be maintained by an ingenious architectural solution, whereby the brothers sat in the choir, while the sisters occupied a kind of mezzanine gallery above them. The brothers' altar would be locasted in the east of the abbey church, the nuns' in the west. Nuns of the order were strictly enclosed, and were to dedicate themselves to meditation and contemplation, with a special devotion to the Blessed Virgin Mary; the brothers ministered to their spiritual needs, but were also expected to preach once a week in the abbey church to the general public. Bridget's visions of the passion and nativity were characteristic of late-medieval devotion to Christ's humanity, and this was reflected in the distinctive dress worn by members of her order. The habit was plain grey, but sisters wore, above their veil and wimple, a cross-shaped crown of white linen onto which were sewn five scraps of red cloth to represent the five wounds of Jesus; the laybrothers' cloaks bore a similar white cross with five red 'drops of blood', while the priest-brothers wore over their hearts a red cross, in the centre of which was a small disc of white cloth, to represent the eucharist.

Bridget obtained a grant of the palace at Vadstena for the building of a monastery soon afterwards, but the process of establishing her order proceeded slowly, and with many obstacles. Her rule for the order was finally given guarded papal approval in 1370, but it was not until after Bridget's death (which took place in Rome in 1373) that the abbey started to become a reality. By the time of the royal party's visit in 1406, however, Vadstena and the Bridgettine order were flourishing. Bridget herself had been canonised by Pope Boniface IX on 7 October 1391. The principal buildings at Vadstena were complete and the abbey could boast a more or less full complement of 85 members. And further houses of the order had started to appear: Paradiso near Florence (founded 1394) with its daughter house Scala Celi in Genoa (1403), and Marienbrunn in Gdansk (Poland, also founded 1394), while preparations were also well advanced for a further foundation at Mariendal near Tallinn (Estonia).

During the stay at Vadstena, Henry FitzHugh appeared before the assembled convent. Expressing the hope 'that the Order called St Saviour's, dedicated to His Mother the Virgin Mary, and subject to the discipline of the Rule mysteriously revealed to the blessed Bridget, His

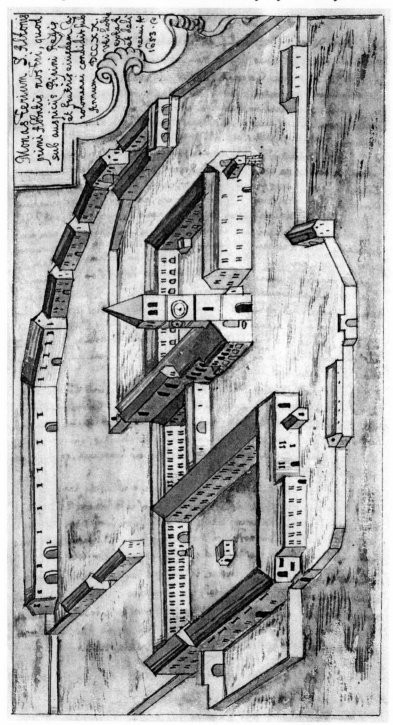

The Bridgettine convent at Altomünster in 1653, showing the church, women's and men's cloisters, and the outer precincts.
Stuttgart, Wuerttembergische Landesbibliothek, HB V 15, fol. 315r.

elect spouse, and situated first in the kingdom of Sweden, at the place called Vadstena, might be established and founded in the kingdom of England', he announced his intention of founding a house of the order. He handed the brothers a charter recording that he had placed the manor of Cherry Hinton, near Cambridge, in trust as the first contribution towards an endowment for the proposed monastery, and he asked that two brothers of Vadstena be sent to England to begin the process of foundation.

It is unlikely that FitzHugh's was a spur-of-the-moment decision. English interest in St Bridget can be traced back to 1348, when she declared her support for Edward III's claim to the throne of France. In 1390 the English Cardinal Adam Easton wrote a treatise arguing the validity of Bridget's revelations, and the following year he was in-volved in the process that led to her canonisation. Manuscript copies of Bridget's voluminous collection of revelations seem to have been available in England before the end of the fourteenth century. And, around the turn of the century, Henry Percy, earl of Northumberland, planned a pilgrimage to Vadstena, though in the event he was detained by service to the crown and was unable to go. It is evident from his charter that FitzHugh had already made legal arrangements for the conveyance of his manor to the Bridgettines before setting off for Swe-den. If, however, he had let Vadstena know of his intentions prior to his visit, there is no record of it. But the proposal was well received. To FitzHugh's announcement and request, it was recorded, 'the brothers assented, with heartfelt joy'.[1]

Accordingly, in the spring of 1408, Vadstena sent the chaplain Mag-nus Hemmingi to England to meet with FitzHugh and discuss the project further. FitzHugh sent Magnus back with a covering letter in which he reassured the mother house that 'I . . . have certainly main-tained my wish and intention as declared to you and written down in your presence at Vadstena'. Henry IV was also brought into the nego-tiations, and wrote his own letter to Vadstena, expressing his delight at the proposed foundation, and declaring his desire 'to be the founder and spiritual protector of this order, and likewise cherish its servants, for the sake of our reverence of God and holy mother Church, in the benevolent and gracious embraces of royal favour'.[2] Even before these letters had been written, the two Vadstena brothers that FitzHugh had requested to help in the process of foundation had set sail from Sweden. Johannes Petri, priest of the order, would spend the next seven years in England, while his younger companion, Katillus Thornberni, deacon, would stay for thirteen.

The pair were well looked after by FitzHugh, at Hinton and elsewhere, but it was a frustrating time. In 1409, plans were drawn up for the Bridgettines to be established in York. They would take over the premises of the hospital of St Nicholas outside Walmgate Bar, which (like many other hospitals in this period) had decayed until it was practically empty, and was earmarked for closure. But, for whatever reason, the plans came to nothing. The last five years of Henry IV's reign saw no real progress. To Henry's existing problems with straitened finances, the distractions of Welsh and Scottish wars, and concerns over religious dissent at home, were added a chronic and debilitating illness that left him unable to exercise personal rule for much of the period. In 1415, seven years after their first arrival, the Vadstena community wrote to Johannes and Katillus expressing sincere worries at their 'long exile in peregrination' and deep compassion for their 'torment and labour', whilst commending their patience, 'which – in such troubled times – has not been conquered by the tedium of expectation, neither has it been vanquished by labour, nor killed by the thunderbolt of desperation.'[3] By this time, however, their fortunes had started to turn.

————•————

When Henry IV died, on 20 March 1413, to be succeeded by his son, contemporaries saw in the new king the chance of a new beginning. Henry V will always be remembered for the French campaigns that he began soon after his accession and, of course, above all the victory at Agincourt, but the new energy and reforming vigour he brought to the kingship were not confined to the military sphere. His government was characterised by an emphasis on good counsel and a professionalisation of the bureaucracy, and he was noted for a rigorous (even strict) sense of justice and the rule of law. In religion, too, he showed a reformer's instincts. At the end of the fourteenth century the English Church had been troubled, almost for the first time, by an outbreak of heresy. The Oxford academic John Wyclif had taught a range of heterodox opinions: that Christ was not really present in the Eucharist, that confession to a priest was not necessary for the forgiveness of sins, that

Contemporary portrait of Henry V.
© National Portrait Gallery, London.

the Bible should be translated into English, the Church disendowed and the monasteries closed. His teachings were condemned, but spread nonetheless. Attempts to crack down on his followers – Wycliffites or 'Lollards' – had been a feature of Henry's father's reign: he enacted the statute *De Haeretico Comburendo* ('For the Burning of Heretics') in 1401, and in 1407 his archbishop of Canterbury, Thomas Arundel, outlined a series of repressive measures against anyone translating the Bible into English, or owning or reading English scriptural texts, or discussing any aspect of Church teaching in the vernacular. With his new archbishop, Henry Chichele, Henry embarked on a more positive programme of orthodox reform: a kind of counter-reformation to set against the proto-Protestantism of Lollardy.

A key element in Henry's promotion of himself as representative of a newly reinvigorated monarchy was what contemporaries described as 'the king's great work at Sheen'. The royal palace at Sheen (later rebuilt as Richmond Palace), on the south (Surrey) bank of the Thames west of London, had been abandoned by Richard II and lay empty throughout the reign of Henry IV. Now Henry conceived an ambitious plan to rebuild it, and to make it the centre of a complex that would combine a royal residence and deerpark with three monastic foundations. Henry chose monasteries of three of the newest religious orders, with a reputation for austerity and spirituality. A little down river from the palace, and the first to be founded, was Sheen Priory, for strictly enclosed and contemplative Carthusian monks. Over the river from the charterhouse, in Isleworth in Middlesex, Henry planned a house of Celestine friars (though in the event, this project never came to fruition). And also on the Middlesex side of the river, in Twickenham, more or less directly across from Sheen Palace, there would be a house of the Bridgettine order.

Shakespeare has popularised the notion that Henry's monastic foundations were made in an attempt to expiate his father's guilt over Richard II's deposition and death (and perhaps, by implication, murder). His Henry, on the morning of Agincourt, prays God to 'think not upon the fault / My father made in compassing the crown', and rehearses the catalogue of good works he has done to try to atone for the sin, culminating with 'I have built / Two chantries, where the sad and solemn priests / Sing still for Richard's soul'.[4] There is no concrete evidence to support the notion, though it does go back to the earliest sources. Whatever the motivation for Henry's foundations, the choice of a Bridgettine house was a good fit from both a spiritual and a worldly perspective. Bridget's contemplative bias and emphasis on the humanity of Jesus accords with what we know of the king's own piety (he was devoted to the Five Wounds of Jesus, for example), while the self-consciously reformist cast of her new order suited Henry's own desire to breathe new life into the monastic institution in England. At the same time, a foundation on the scale of a Bridgettine monastery, which was moreover an order previously unknown in England, was an ideal way for Henry to announce his arrival as an impressive and ambitious monarch. We may assume that Henry lord FitzHugh, who by now had risen to be chamberlain of the royal household, took every opportunity to press the Bridgettine case.

King Henry laid the foundation stone for the new monastery himself, in a ceremony presided over by the bishop of London, on 22 February 1415. On 3 March at Westminster he issued the foundation charter of 'the Monastery of St Saviour and St Bridget of Syon', with FitzHugh one of the witnesses. This is the first official appearance of the name 'Syon', though there is some evidence that it was under consideration as long ago as 1409, when the establishment of a house at York was being mooted. Syon is the biblical Zion, the site of Solomon's temple and the city of David, and a synonym in the Middle Ages for Jerusalem. It made an obvious pair with Henry's companion foundation of Sheen (founded the previous year), whose full name was 'The Charterhouse of Jesus of Bethlehem of Sheen', and indeed Henry was said to have founded Syon 'in honour of the resurrection of our lord Jesus Christ'.[5] The charter is a lengthy document, containing a mix of piety, legal precision, and an urge to micro-manage the affairs of his new foundation that (as we shall see presently) led to some complications later. Henry explicitly sees the foundation as cementing his kingly identity, as he follows in the footsteps of the 'kings and princes and our most renowned progenitors' who had founded monasteries in the past, and he required prayers from the inmates in perpetuity 'for our healthful estate while we live, and for our soul when we shall have departed this life, and for the souls of our most dear lord and father Henry, late king of England, and Mary his late wife, our most dear mother; also for the souls of John late duke of Lancaster our grandfather, and Blanch his late wife our grandmother, and of our other progenitors, and of all the faithful deceased'.[6] For all the piety, there is politics here too, as any discontinuity between the royal line of English 'kings and princes' and the house of Lancaster is quietly glossed over.

Syon was endowed with estates across England, from Kent in the east to St Michael's Mount off the Cornish coast, and as far north as Lancashire and Lincolnshire. Much of the property had formerly belonged to the alien priories (that is, religious houses that were subordinate outposts of foreign – generally French – abbeys); in a populist move, they had been dissolved, and their lands confiscated, in the previous year. In case the new owners should have any difficulty securing the estates and drawing the income from them, Henry underwrote the endowment from the Exchequer in the sum of 1000 marks (£666 13s. 4d.) per annum (a mark was two thirds of a pound). At a stroke, Syon became the richest nunnery in England, and one of the wealthiest of all English monasteries.

Shortly after issuing the foundation charter, Henry wrote to Vadstena, informing the community there of his foundation, and telling them that the new monastery 'is under construction and hastens towards completion' (which was probably overstating the case somewhat). He asked them to send one of the brothers and six of the more experienced sisters from Vadstena, 'so that they will be able to instruct those, who in the future come to join this sacred order, in the observances and rules of the order'.[7] As it happens, the mother house was already significantly committed to a number of other foundations in process around Europe, and had to be leaned on not only by Henry, but by his sister Philippa and her husband Erik, the king and queen of Sweden, before they sent a party to England. Its composition was not exactly as requested by Henry: the priest-brother Johannes Johannis of Kalmar was accompanied by four sisters, three novices and Magnus Hemmingi, who was not a professed Bridgettine but a chaplain attached to Vadstena. (We have seen already that he visited England in 1408, at the beginning of the process that led finally to the foundation of 1415.)

What kind of community, and what kind of settlement, they found on their arrival at Twickenham at the end of summer 1415 is not quite known. Stone had started to arrive from Yorkshire, and other building materials were supplied from the site at Sheen. Presumably there was accommodation and a chapel. In the absence of any Bridgettine tradition in England, Henry's hope was that members of the existing religious orders would decide to migrate to the new foundation, but though some had probably arrived there were as yet no professed Bridgettine nuns or brothers. And there were the superiors-designate of the new monastery, the abbess Matilda (or Maud) Newton and the confessor general William Alnwick. Almost immediately, however, things began to go badly wrong, and neither Newton nor Alnwick would ever be professed as Bridgettines of Syon.

Historians disagree about the origins of these problems. Was there something in Newton and Alnwick's characters and leadership style that led to the conflict? Were there structural weaknesses in their appointment that inevitably undermined their positions from the outset? Or were the issues that arose part of wider problems in the Bridgettine order? It may be that all three factors were involved. We have no contemporary testimony as to their personal characteristics, but it is possible to say that neither Alnwick nor Newton had the extensive leadership experience one might expect for such key appointments. He had been a recluse, she an ordinary nun of Barking Abbey. Their roles as Syon's superiors were, moreover, somewhat anomalous. The abbess and confessor general were supposed to be elected by the members of the monastic community, but of course at the time of the foundation there was as yet no community to elect them. In such circumstances it was usual to appoint a caretaker administration: that is what had happened at Vadstena in the years immediately preceding the election of the first abbess, and at Sheen John Widdrington was appointed 'rector' in 1414 before being confirmed as the first prior in 1417, when the monastery was formally consecrated. But Henry had nominated Newton and Alnwick as abbess and confessor general from the start. In a letter to the pope from around this time, Henry allowed the possibility that 'errors may have been committed in the foundation of Syon, or in the manner of the reception of religious to that monastery.'[8] The Swedish sisters, in particular, may have been uncomfortable rendering obedience to superiors who were not themselves professed members of the order, and were presumably still feeling their way into the Bridgettine way of life. The relationship between the two superiors seems also to have been strained, though this was not a problem unique to Syon. Indeed the division of spiritual and temporal authority between the abbess and confessor general was a vexed question throughout the order, and remained so into the seventeenth century. Finally, the sisters from Vadstena brought with them to England a more specific dispute that was currently preoccupying the mother house. In her rule, Bridget had not made provision for laysisters. The omission was unusual. Did she intend that the nuns of the monastery should perform manual work for themselves? The majority of Vadstena nuns were of aristocratic origin, unused to such occupations, and unwilling to start. In time, a reinterpretation of Bridget's original intentions would see the introduction of laysisters to the order. But at Syon in the autumn of 1415, the result was a crisis of authority.

Henry V was, as we know, otherwise engaged when all this blew up: the battle of Agincourt was fought on 25 October (St Crispin's day, as Shakespeare reminds us), and he was not back in London until about a month later. But he could not allow his flagship foundation to descend into faction and chaos. In January 1416 he convened a crisis meeting. Henry himself joined the discussions, which were attended by the entire body of brothers and nuns, plus a committee of experts, comprising the bishop of St David's, two experienced monks (the abbot of St Alban's and the prior of Coventry), two leading academic theologians, and Thomas Fishbourne, a St Alban's recluse and confidant of the king. (If Fishbourne's qualifications for the assignment are less obvious than those of his fellow committee members, his importance in the next phase of Syon's history will become apparent in the next few pages.) News of the arguments reached the Vadstena community, who wrote in a letter of 'the great sorrows and anxieties' they felt at the dispute, in which 'our brothers made assertions against the sisters, and the sisters against the statement of the brothers.'[9] But in the end agreement was reached. The nuns should expect to carry out manual work, as their sisters at Vadstena did, and the abbess did indeed have to defer to the confessor general in spiritual matters. Not long afterwards, Matilda Newton was relieved of her duties as abbess by the king and returned to Barking to live as a recluse, whilst William Alnwick, 'worn out by age and weariness', it was said, went back to the solitude of his cell.

Temporary leadership of the community was assumed on the women's side by the Swedish sisters, and among the brothers by Thomas Fishbourne. (No doubt it was with this role in mind that Henry had brought him into the discussions in 1416.) Henry's foundation was confirmed by the pope in 1418 and, at last, everything was ready for the community to be formally enclosed. On 21 April 1420, the archbishop of Canterbury, Henry Chichele, conducted a ceremony in which he received the professions of twenty-seven sisters, five priests, two deacons and three laybrothers as members of the Order of St Saviour. The community must have proceeded quite quickly to choose its first canonically elected superiors, because on 5 May the bishop of London, Richard Clifford, wrote to Henry V to report that he had confirmed the election of Joan North, previously a nun of Markyate in Hertfordshire, as abbess, and Thomas Fishbourne as confessor general, 'the which persons I trust, by God's grace, shall much profit in that place, in that holy company both of men and of women, the which God of his mercy grant'.[10] Henry FitzHugh's vision, first conceived some fifteen years earlier, of an English house of the Bridgettine order, had become reality.

Notes

[1.] Documents quoted by Margaret Deanesly, *The Incendium Amoris of Richard Rolle of Hampole* (Manchester: Manchester University Press, 1915), pp. 97–8.

[2.] Elin Andersson, 'Birgittines in Contact: Early Correspondence between England and Vadstena', *Eranos* 102 (2004), 1–29, pp. 13, 14.

[3.] *Ibid.*, p. 18.

[4.] *Henry V*, Act IV, scene i.

[5.] According to the *Syon Martiloge* (British Library, Add. MS 22285), fol. 14v.

[6.] G. J. Aungier, *The History and Antiquities of Syon Monastery, the Parish of Isleworth, and the Chapelry of Hounslow* (London: J. B. Nichols & Son, 1840), pp. 25–30.

[7.] Andersson, 'Birgittines in Contact', p. 15.

[8.] Deanesly, *Incendium Amoris*, p. 128.

[9.] *Ibid.*, p. 112.

[10.] *Ibid.*, p. 129.

2

✤ *Medieval Syon* ✤

ALTHOUGH SYON WAS NOW SAFELY ESTABLISHED, the new community faced a number of significant difficulties in these early years. Some were local; others general to the Bridgettine order as a whole. First, little more than two years after the the formal enclosure, in August 1422, the abbey's founder and patron, Henry V, died, to be succeeded by his infant son, Henry VI, who was just nine months old. The abbess, along with the other great landholders of the realm, had to begin the process of procuring confirmations of the abbey's title to its possessions. Letters of confirmation were finally issued in 1424.

Meanwhile, the Bridgettine order as a whole had found its very existence threatened by papal decree. The origins of the controversy lie in a dispute within the order's Italian houses over the status and constitutional position of the brothers. In 1422, under the influence of the dissident party, the pope, Martin V, issued his so-called Bull of Separation in which he ordered all double monasteries to disaggregate, and form two separate convents, one for men and one for women. The requirement struck at the very heart of St Bridget's vision. The order almost immediately began to petition Pope Martin to revoke the bull, and in the summer of 1423 Syon's confessor general, Thomas Fishbourne, left for Rome. Arriving in August, he met the pope several times, recruited some of the top legal experts at the papal curia, and drew up a detailed submission pointing out the unintended consequences of the bull for the Bridgettine order. Following extensive legal argument, in November the pope agreed to exempt Syon from the Bull of Separation. Soon afterwards he did the same for the Scandinavian monasteries. Fishbourne remained in Rome until 1425, when he also secured from the pope a confirmation (published in the bull *Mare Anglicanum*) that all the rights and privileges of the Bridgettine order granted earlier in the century should also apply to Syon, as well as several valuable indulgences.

Above. Location of Syon House, Isleworth, by the Thames.
Detail from Moses Glover's map of Isleworth hundred, 1635.
The Archives of the Duke of Northumberland at Syon House, Sy: B.XIII.
© Collections of the Duke of Northumberland.

Right. Plan of Syon Abbey, Isleworth, based on excavations at Syon Park.
MOLA (Museum of London Archaeology).

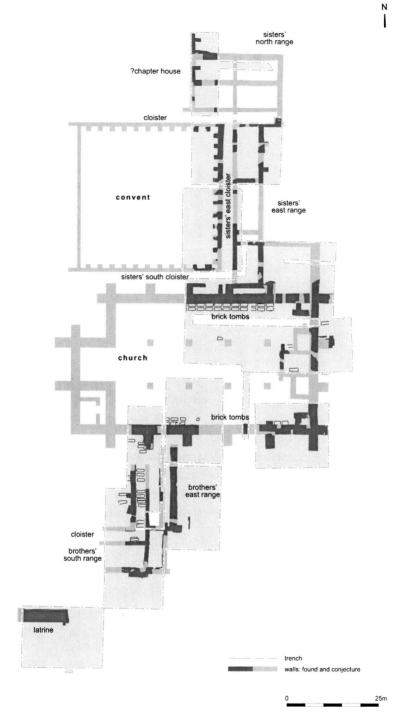

N

sisters'
north range

?chapter house

cloister

convent

sisters' east cloister

sisters'
east range

sisters' south cloister

brick tombs

church

brick tombs

brothers'
east range

cloister

brothers'
south range

latrine

trench

walls: found and conjecture

0   25m

All through this period, the Syon community had been growing. Thirty-seven men and women had made their professions in 1420; by 1428 (the year for which we next have a full list of members) the community numbered fifty-five. Under pressure of numbers their accommodation had started to become cramped. It had also become apparent that the Twickenham site was marshy and unhealthy. The decision was taken to relocate a few miles down river to the site in Isleworth where Syon House now stands, and which Henry V had probably originally intended for his house of Celestines. The foundation stone for the church of the new monastery was laid on 5 February 1426, in the presence of the regent, John duke of Bedford, and another key member of the ruling council, Henry Cardinal Beaufort, bishop of Winchester. Five years later building was far enough advanced for the move to take place, and on 11 November 1431, in a ceremony conducted by Henry Chichele, the archbishop of Canterbury who had presided over the first professions, the community was solemnly re-enclosed and could settle into life at its new and (so they assumed) permanent site.

———

The life of a Syon nun was a demanding one. The point was impressed on all potential new recruits to the Bridgettine order. On their first visit to the monastery, the abbess was to warn them of 'the hardness of the religious life, that is to say, contempt of the world, forgetting of father and mother and all worldly friendship, except insofar as the rule allows and the Church determines, much fasting, many water days, long vigils, early risings, long services in Choir, daily labour, strict silence, lowest place, hard commandments from their superiors, prompt obedience, giving up of their own will, patience in adversity, putting up with all sharp corrections, and many other such things'.[1] This, and much of our other information about daily life at Syon, comes from the *Syon Additions for the Sisters*, a detailed supplement to St Bridget's *Rule of St Saviour* that was drawn up as a record of customary practice at the monastery around the middle of the fifteenth century. (The corresponding *Additions* for the laybrothers are also extant, although those for the priest-brothers have unfortunately not survived.)

A Bridgettine monastery, as the debates of 1423 had helped to clarify, was made up of two convents, one for men and one for women. At Syon the brothers' cloister and associated buildings were probably sited to the south of the abbey church, and the nuns' to the north. In the church the two groups were kept separate, and indeed invisible to each other, by the unique 'double-decker' arrangement of the choir described in Chapter One. The nuns lived under strict enclosure. The door to their cloister was secured with two locks, the two keys to which were kept in two strong chests, one on the brothers' side, one on the sisters'. Each chest had three locks, and the three different keys required to open them were in the keeping of the abbess and two sisters on the nuns' side, and the confessor general and two of the brothers, on the other. When an item needed to be passed from one side to the other, rather than open the door, the community made use of 'the wheel' – a revolving device set in the wall that allowed the transfer to be made without one group seeing the other, or being seen. The nuns made their confessions to the brothers at a window covered with a grate, which (like the modern confessional grille) allowed them to be heard but not seen. The windows could be opened for the sisters to take communion, which they generally did on the major festivals, though by special licence of the confessor general they could communicate once a week, on a Saturday. Visitors might be received on Sunday afternoons, and on major feast days. They came to the grates, so that the nuns normally remained invisible to them, though exceptions might be made: 'if in case any desire to be seen of their father, mother, or honest dear friends, they may open the window by leave of the abbess'. The abbess, however, 'shall not lightly grant this but seldom in the year'; and, moreover, the *Rule* continues, 'if they open not the window a more plenteous reward is promised them in times to come'.[2]

The sisters slept in the dorter or dormitory, a single building partitioned into separate cells for each of the fifty-nine sisters (the abbess had her own room). In common with all monastic communities in the Christian tradition, their day was dominated by the divine office or recitation of the canonical hours. They broke their sleep soon after midnight for the night office of matins, then rose at dawn, to begin the day with lauds; prime was sung at about 6 am; terce, at 9 am, sext, at noon; none (despite the name) followed at 3 pm, vespers or evensong at 6 pm, and compline before bed around 9 pm. The sisters began their services as soon as the brothers finished theirs, so that, near enough, Syon fulfilled the Pauline ideal of prayer without ceasing (see 1 Thess.

5: 17). Each day after prime a mass of the Blessed Virgin Mary was celebrated by one of the priests. Terce began as soon as the mass had finished, meaning that the nuns were in church from 6 am until at least 10 am. Then, after terce, the sisters went in procession to the cemetery, where an open grave was always kept ready. At the grave-side they recited the *De profundis* (Psalm 130, part of the Office of the Dead), prayed for the strength to keep their bodies pure until the day of their death, and marked the obits of any members of the community whose anniversary fell that day. A bier with a little earth sprinkled on it also lay at the entrance of the church, 'where it may always be seen of them that enter, that seeing it they may have in mind the remembrance of death, and think in their hearts that they be earth and to earth they shall return.'[3]

After the observances at the grave were complete the nuns, for the first time in the day, were permitted to speak to each other if they wished. They could speak also between the hours and other timetabled activities for the remainder of the day, although strict silence was to be maintained in the church, cloister, frater or refectory, dorter, toilets, washing house and library. At those times and in those places where conversation was permitted, the sisters' speech was to be 'meek and low, soft and demure, sweet and true, ever of spiritual things, and concerning matters strictly necessary according to the rule, delighting ever rather to hear and be still than to speak.'[4] Otherwise, communication was allowed only by hand signals. Such systems of signs were usual among the stricter monastic orders, in which lengthy silences were enjoined. Syon's medieval *Book of Signs* survives, and provides a list of 106 gestures to signify a range of essential terms, including the names of people (for *abbess*, 'make the sign for age and also for a woman'); places (for *cloister*, 'make a round circle with your right forefinger toward the earth'); objects such as candles, books, items of clothing; foodstuff and condiments (for *mustard*, 'hold your nose in the upper part of your right fist and rub it'); activities (for *sleeping*, 'put your right hand under your cheek and with that close your eyes'), and basic expressions such as 'good', 'straight away', 'I don't know', or 'enough.'[5]

Every Thursday after tierce the abbess (or another senior officer in her place) presided over the chapter, at which the community came together to review the past week, for individual nuns to acknowledge any faults they may have committed and for penances to be assigned. Sisters were expected to own up to their failings themselves; if another had to accuse them, then the penance was doubled. Faults ranged from the less serious – arriving late for choir, say, or with one's habit incomplete; to the more serious – insubordination, threatening to strike another, questioning the validity of the revelations of St Bridget; to the most serious, including fornication, open rebellion, or murder. Penances ranged from the imposition of certain prayers and additional silences, to corporal punishment. There was even, for the most grievous offences, a prison within the monastery.

There were two meals a day. Dinner followed the canonical hour of none (so, about 4 pm), and supper followed evensong, at around 7 pm. The nuns abstained from meat in Lent and Advent, at certain other prescribed times in the year, and every Wednesday, Friday and Saturday. On a number of specified solemnities and vigils they fasted to bread and water. The usual drink was beer. (Monastic beer was only weakly alcoholic – and, since its manufacture included boiling, it was a much safer drink than untreated water.) Meals were taken communally in the frater, and in silence. They were accompanied by readings from edifying sources including the *Rule of St Augustine*, *Rule of St Saviour*, and the *Syon Additions to the Rule*. The day ended with another reading, while the sisters took their collation or bedtime drink. The abbess chose 'some spiritual matter of ghostly edification, to help to gather together the scatterings of the mind from all outward things' and to keep them 'in inward peace and stableness of mind all the night following.'[6]

Such free time as their daily routine allowed, the nuns spent either working – in the garden, or at embroidery, for example – or reading. The fifteenth century was a time of rapidly developing literacy. Whereas earlier in the Middle Ages the ability to read would have been an accomplishment unnecessary to many and possessed by very few, now a certain level of literacy was relatively common in aristocractic circles, and perhaps especially in gentry and merchant households. Syon nuns were expected to be able to read English, and at least to follow their Latin servicebooks. For those who did not understand Latin, a translation and commentary on the Bridgettine office, entitled *The Mirror of Our Lady*, was provided – probably by one of the brothers – early in the abbey's history. Over and above their liturgical obligations, however,

Office of the Dead, with prayer for the soul of 'King Henry, our founder'.
Exeter University Library MS 262/2, fol. 168v.

the sisters valued personal reading. As *The Mirror of Our Lady* puts it: 'Like as in prayer, man speaks to God; so in reading, God speaks to man'.[7] Although Bridget's *Rule* was notably strict on the acquisition and retention of property by houses of the order, the sisters were allowed to collect as many books as they wished for learning or study. We know that they had a library, though unfortunately its catalogue does not survive. (The catalogue of the brothers' library will be discussed in the next section.) Those surviving books that can be linked to Syon indicate an interest in works of devotion and contemplation: among them, the English mystical authors Richard Rolle and Walter Hilton, and the *Imitation of Christ* by Thomas Kempis.

More than half the sixty nuns held some position of responsibility in the monastic organisation, such as librarian, infirmaress, keeper of the wheel or grates, or an assistant to one of the principal officers. There were six of these, besides the abbess. The prioress was the latter's deputy, and took her place whenever she was absent. She was also responsible for maintaining strict observance of the rule among the nuns, and in this she was assisted by four or more 'searchers': senior sisters who – rather like school prefects – were her eyes and ears around the convent. The treasuress handled all the monastery's income from its estates, maintained the accounts, and had safekeeping of the abbey's charters and other documents. The cellaress bought in all necessary provisions for the monastery, supervised the production of food and drink on site (baking, brewing, etc.), and managed the household servants. The chamberess was responsible for the provision and repair of habits and other clothing, bedding, and all related items. The sexton or sacristan was in charge of the church furnishings: chalices and other ornaments, altar-cloths and the like, oil and wax for lamps, and everything else required for services in the abbey church. Finally, the chantress man-aged the performance of divine service, supervising the arrangement of the choirs; providing, repairing, and if necessary correcting service books, and so on.

It is worth pausing to emphasise the extent of these officers' roles. In an age that gave women few rights, and trusted them with little responsibility, these were significant leadership positions, not least in the context of a double monastery. The treasuress – and not one of the brothers – oversaw the whole of the abbey's income and expenditure, for example, and the cellaress was responsible for the provisioning of the entire community. And above them all was the abbess, whose authority was final in every aspect of the monastery's governance except for those spiritual matters that were reserved to the confessor general. To find a woman as chief executive of a major institution, itself part of a multi-national corporation, holding vast estates, managing an annual income of some £2000 (perhaps £1m in today's money), a community of eighty-five women and men plus a numerous staff of professional administrators, lawyers and servants, is certainly surprising for the Middle Ages, and perhaps for some later periods too.

What kinds of women were the nuns of Syon Abbey? The popular notion that nunneries were full of the unmarried and unmarriageable daughters of the aristocracy is some way from the truth, certainly for the late Middle Ages. Even so fashionable and well-connected an establishment as Syon became was dominated by members of the gentry and merchant classes. We can see this pattern emerging, for example, in the list of forty sisters who witnessed the election of Robert Bell as the second confessor general, following the death of Thomas Fishbourne, in 1428. Providing a direct connection to the monastery's foundation were the half dozen Swedish women who had arrived from Vadstena in 1415. A number of sisters shared with Syon's founder Henry FitzHugh a northern origin. They included Anne Bowes, daughter of a prominent merchant family in York, and Joan and Isabel Fishbourne, probably kin to the late confessor general, and from Fishbourn (Co. Durham). The community included other family groups, most notably Margaret, Katherine and Joan Suckling, who were probably sisters of the prioress, Juliana Suckling. They were from a gentry family of lesser landowners in Isleworth, and thus Syon's neighbours. Matilda Muston's family also held lands locally in Middlesex. They were merchants who had made their money in the export trade. Matilda succeeded Joan North as abbess in 1433, and later in the fifteenth century Elizabeth and Agnes Muston also became nuns of Syon. Elena Wyche was from a prominent family of mercers in London, while Emma Sevenoak was related to William Sevenoak, lord mayor in 1418–19. He had also been appointed a supervisor of the building work on the new monastery at Isleworth in 1426. Other sisters had connections with the court. The families of Philippa Arundel, Margaret Ashby, Margery Philips and Katherine

Stook were all in the service of Henry V. Later in the century they would be joined by a few members of noble families, and a number of women who came from the affinities of some of Syon's high-ranking aristocratic patrons, such as Margaret Holland, duchess of Clarence, or her grand-daughter Margaret Beaufort (who is discussed later in the chapter).

Women could not be professed younger than eighteen and this, combined with a year-long novitiate that was, unusually, spent outside the monastic enclosure, seems to have resulted in well-tested vocations and few if any mistakes in admission. One or two brothers found the life harder than they had expected and were permitted to leave, but among the nuns, the only question mark hangs over Joanna Sewell. She was accepted as a novice near the end of the fifteenth century, and was apparently assigned for instruction to the Carthusian monk James Grenehalgh of Sheen, on the opposite side of the river. He was a book-lover, and annotated the books that he and Sewell read together sometimes with his intials, sometimes with hers, and sometimes with both sets of initials intertwined. Whether the entanglement went any further than that is not certain, but he was disciplined by his order and sent away, writing 'Forsake Sewell' in the margin of one of his books. She remained at Syon, making her profession in 1500, and remained there until her death in 1532.

Brothers of the Bridgettine order existed primarily to provide spiritual services to the nuns: to hear their confessions, to administer the eucharist to them and to bury them when they were dead. As we have seen, they were excluded from the management of the monastery and its estates, which were entirely the responsibility of the abbess and the officers she appointed from among the sisters. Their day took its shape and rhythm from the divine office. They were bound to the recitation of the canonical hours, though, unlike the sisters, for whom Bridget had composed a special office, they followed the use of the diocese in which the monastery was situated (in Syon's case, the use of St Paul's, or London diocese). High mass was celebrated daily, after the sisters had finished their hour of sext, at about 1 pm.

Like the sisters, they lived under strict enclosure: only the eremitic Carthusian order was stricter on this point. There are, however, a few cases of recorded absence when the affairs of the monastery required it. We have already seen that Thomas Fishbourne travelled to Rome in response to the emergency of the early 1420s, when he was accompanied by the priest-brother Simon Winter. In 1427 Robert Bell and the deacon Thomas Sterrington were absent from Syon for six months on a visit to the mother house at Vadstena, where they presented an exhaustive list of questions on aspects of the Bridgettine rule. In one respect, however, the brothers were significantly more outward-facing than the sisters. St Bridget required them to preach publicly in the abbey church on all major feast days, and to give a sermon in English on the gospel of the day during mass every Sunday. It was a duty the community took seriously: a brother who was scheduled to preach was excused from divine service for three days in order to prepare his sermon and commit it to memory. The sermons seem to have been well attended, and the brothers would also often hear the confessions of members of the public as part of their visit.

The Bridgettine Rule stipulated that no brother could be professed before the age of twenty-five. (Other orders accepted candidates in their late teens.) This meant that men generally arrived with a considerable quantity and range of life-experience. Thomas Fishbourne, for example, had been an esquire (and perhaps married), a member of the household of the bishop of Durham, steward of St Albans abbey in Hertfordshire, and a hermit, before his profession at Syon. In general, the social profile of recruits is not dissimilar to that of the sisters, in that postulants tended to come from the lesser landholding families of Middlesex, and from the London merchant elite. (Most of the lay-brothers were also local men, though – in contrast to their counterparts in the great Cistercian houses, for example – they were not necessarily unlettered labourers. One had been a successful lawyer before receiving his vocation; several donated books to the brothers' library.) A number of Syon's priests had served London parishes before entering the abbey, and several had resigned valuable livings in order to do so. The London priests Thomas Westhawe and John Pinchbeck were both celebrated preachers before they joined Syon in the mid-fifteenth century. Pinchbeck found the Bridgettine life tough, and was subsequently granted permission to transfer to a less strict order, but Westhawe went on to be elected the third confessor general in 1472.

Westhawe is also representative of a class of university graduates and career academics who were increasingly drawn to Syon as the Middle Ages went on. Among the men present in 1428 at Robert Bell's election, only one was a graduate. John Bracebridge was an Oxford MA who came to Syon, probably as one of the first professions in 1420, after a thirty-year career as a schoolmaster in Lincolnshire. By contrast, in the sixteenth century more than half of the priests and deacons had attended one of the universities, and half of these had gone on to an academic career. Westshawe was a Cambridge Doctor of Theology and fellow of Pembroke Hall from 1436 until at least 1446. Two sixteenth-century confessors general, Stephen Sander and John Fewterer, had also previously been fellows of Pembroke. Earlier, the lawyer John Dodd was a fellow of New College, Oxford, in the 1450s and 1460s before being professed at Syon, and Richard Terenden followed a similar route a decade or so later. The sixteenth-century priests also included Richard Whitford, who had studied at the University of Paris and befriended Erasmus before taking up his fellowship at Queen's College Cambridge, and Richard Reynolds, of Corpus Christi College, Cambridge, who was widely recognised as one of the greatest scholars of the age. Their intellectual interests and achievements (and Reynolds's martyrdom) will feature in the next chapter.

Men such as these must have been attracted by, and in their turn helped to shape, the Syon brothers' library, which grew to be one of the great intellectual resources of late-medieval England. Its foundations had been laid by John Bracebridge, who brought with him on his profession his collection of over a hundred volumes on a wide range of subjects, not only the classics and grammar textbooks associated with his previous career as a schoolmaster, but works on science and medicine, theology, and devotional treatises. (Instead of Bracebridge, Henry V might have been regarded as the founder of the Syon library. He had left many of his books, including all those useful for preaching the gospel, to Syon but, for reasons that remain mysterious, the terms of his will in this regard were never carried out.) The collection grew steadily, as new recruits donated their books, augmented by further gifts from outside benefactors, commissions, and purchases on the second-hand market. By the second half of the fifteenth century, the Syon brothers already had an enviable library, especially strong in biblical scholarship, the Church fathers, academic texts in the scholastic tradition, devotional works and aids to sermon composition, as well as classical literature, philosophy and medicine.

And then, under confessor general Thomas Westhawe, the library underwent an overhaul. In 1479 there were major alterations to the library buildings. From 1482, Syon retained the services of Thomas Baille, a scribe and bookbinder, with the express purpose of keeping its books in the best possible condition. And, at about the same date, Thomas Betson, a Cambridge-educated lawyer and formerly rector of Wimbish in Essex, joined the Syon community as one of its four deacons, and was appointed keeper of the library. The changes to library provision were almost certainly prompted by changes in technology. During the 1470s printed books started to appear in England, and Syon quickly established itself in the forefront of the acquisition of books from the continental presses. Over the next twenty years the collection grew to over 1300 volumes, all of which were meticulously recorded by Betson in a catalogue that is one of the fullest and most detailed of any that survive from medieval England. Even before its expansion the brothers' library was a rich resource: Thomas Gascoigne, for example, chancellor of Oxford University in the 1440s and 1450s, was a regular visitor to the abbey to consult the books held there. But by the sixteenth century, the addition of substantial numbers of books representing the 'new learning' of renaissance humanism had given Syon one of the largest, and most up-to-date, libraries in England. We will return to its shelves in the next chapter.

So far, this chapter has painted a world of quiet contemplation and silent study. But there was another side to Syon Abbey in the Middle Ages. For one thing, it was, for much of the fifteenth century, a construction site. Although the community had taken up residence at Isleworth in 1431, building was by no means complete. The records are intermittent (as they usually are for the Middle Ages), but we know that work was ongoing in 1443, when safe passage was granted for workmen and materials. Between 1461 and 1479 expenditure on building ran at between £400 and £500 a year (or a quarter of the abbey's income). In the year 1501–2, when almost £600 was spent, materials included 125 loads of stone, 104,000 bricks, 49,500 tiles and nearly 26,000 feet of timber board. Stone was brought by water to the abbey's own wharf on the Thames: timber was set aside for repairs to the wharf itself in 1501–2, and the crane was mended in 1518. Bricks were made on site which, together with the dressing of stone and the sawing of timber, can only have contributed to the dust, fumes and noise of the monastery precincts. It has been estimated that the number of men employed on the project during the main phases of building cannot have been less than one hundred at any time. Nor was the abbey church complete by this date: it was not ready for consecration until 20 October 1488. Even then, construction continued at barely reduced intensity for another twenty years, before the monastery was apparently complete, some one hundred years after its first foundation.

Much of the new building in the late fifteenth century seems to have been designed to cater for pilgrims to the abbey. Syon was an important centre for pilgrimage. Although it could never rival St Thomas Becket's shrine at Canterbury or Our Lady of Walsingham, in the sixteenth century its income from offerings was reckoned to be the fourth highest in England. Pilgrims could receive indulgences (that is, remission of a portion of the penalty due to be paid for sin in Purgatory) of varying amounts for visiting the monastery and contributing to its building and upkeep, for being present at one of the brothers' sermons, or for prayers and offerings at certain shrines in the abbey church, notably that of St Bridget. Generous indulgences were available on particular days, including many of the major feasts. The greatest attraction for pilgrims, however, was the Vincula indulgence. This offered visitors to the abbey on the feast of St Peter ad Vincula (Peter in Chains, 1 August, which was also known as Lammas day) and during the week following, providing they were suitably penitent and confessed, plenary remission: that is, release from the pains of Purgatory due for all the sins they had committed in their life up to that point. (There were a very few, extremely serious exceptions, such as killing a priest.) The so-called 'Syon Pardon' was immensely popular. Margery Kempe was at Syon at Lammastide in 1434 'to obtain her pardon through the mercy of our Lord,'[8] and the poet John Awdelay wrote a carol in praise of St Bridget that doubles as an advertisement for the indulgence. Alongside the spiritual benefits they had accrued, visitors could bring away a tangible memento. All medieval pilgrimage sites did a trade in souvenirs (palms from Jerusalem, cockleshells from Santiago de Compostela). Pilgrim badges from Syon depict St Bridget, usually with an angel perched on her shoulder to signify the divine inspiration of her revelations, sometimes in a canopy to represent the monastery, sometimes with a mirror attached. Devotional images could be purchased and, later, so could printed books and pamphlets connected with the abbey.

The outer precincts of the abbey, then, were thronging with pilgrims and workmen, scholars there to use the library and sellers of souvenirs. Here, too, were the monastic bakery, the brewhouse, grain mill, coal store, and slaughterhouse. There was accommodation for guests. King Henry VI maintained his own chamber in the abbey precincts. Soon after the move to Isleworth he had received special papal permission to enter the nuns' enclosure, provided he came in the company of two bishops and two noblemen aged over fifty, and that he stayed for no longer than three hours at a time.[9] There were numerous other aristocratic visitors. We will see in the next chapter that Katherine of Aragon and her daughter, the Princess Mary, often took a boat across the Thames from the royal palace of Richmond to Syon. Lady Margaret Beaufort, the mother of Henry VII, was a regular visitor to the nuns, and she too had papal permission to enter the enclosure. One of her protegés was Margaret Pole, daughter of George duke of Clarence and mother of Cardinal Reginald Pole; she was widowed in 1504 and resided in the abbey precincts at least between 1505 and 1509.

Other pious widows were attracted into Syon's spiritual orbit. Susan Kyngeston was born Susan Fettyplace, of the Fettyplace family of Besselsleigh, Berkshire. Her husband John died soon after their marriage, in 1514, and, instead of remarrying, she chose to take a vow of perpetual chastity. The life of a vowess was recognised as a religious vocation in the late Middle Ages. Women (usually widows) took vows before the bishop, and received a distinctive mantle and a ring in recognition that they were married now to Christ. Some continued to live in the family home, but some attached themselves to religious houses. Susan Kyngeston is recorded at Syon between 1514 and 1537. She was joined there for a time in the 1520s by her grandmother, Alice Beselles, who had also vowed chastity after her own husband's death. Around the same time, Susan's younger sisters, Dorothy Goodrington (herself recently widowed) and the unmarried Eleanor Fettyplace, decided to enter Syon itself as professed sisters. They remained nuns of Syon until the suppression of the monastery, and beyond, and we shall meet them again in a subsequent chapter.

Notes

1.   James Hogg, *The Rewyll of Seynt Sauioure and Other Middle English Brigittine Legislative Texts. Volume 4: The Syon Additions for the Sisters* (Salzburg: Institut für Anglistik und Amerikanistik Universität Salzburg, 1980), p. 80.

2.   'Rule of Our Most Holy Saviour', ch. 7, in *Rule of Our Most Holy Saviour and the Additions* (?Plymouth, 1914); and *Syon Additions for the Sisters*, p. 75.

3.   'Rule of Our Most Holy Saviour', ch. 24.

4.   *Syon Additions for the Sisters*, p. 73

5.   Hogg, *The Rewyll of Seynt Sauioure. Voume 3: The Syon Additions for the Brethren and The Boke of Sygnes*, pp. 134–44.

6.   *The Myroure of Oure Ladye*, ed. John Henry Blunt, Early English Text Society, Extra Series 19 (London: N. Trübner & Co., 1873), p. 165.

7.   *Ibid.*, p. 66.

8.   Book II, ch. 10, trans. Barry Windeatt, *The Book of Margery Kempe* (Harmondsworth: Penguin, 1985), p. 290.

9.   *Calendar of Papal Registers Relating to Great Britain and Ireland, Volume 8, 1427–1447*, ed. J. A. Twemlow (London: HMSO, 1909), pp. 617–18.

3

✣ The Road to Exile ✣

A CHAPTER that will take us to the Tower and Tyburn, before it concludes with the community turned out of their convent and facing an uncertain future, begins in the quiet of the Syon Abbey library. Richard Pace was a brilliant scholar, a diplomat and a courtier. He had studied with the great humanist teachers of Padua, Bologna and Ferrara, and established a close friendship with Erasmus. During the first half of the 1510s he was engaged in diplomatic service principally in Rome and Venice, and later became secretary to Henry VIII and a trusted confidant. In 1518 he succeeded John Colet as Dean of St Paul's. But he was also plagued by what we would think of as a chronic depressive illness, and periodically had to withdraw from public life. He spent substantial amounts of time in the 1520s sequestered away from the pressures of the court and its intrigues in lodgings at Syon Abbey. There he was visited, in July 1527, by Gasparo Spinelli, secretary to the Venetian ambassador to England. Spinelli described his meeting in a letter to his brother: 'I have been at Syon visiting the reverend Pace, who is leading the life of the blessed in that lovely spot. Arrayed in his clerical garb, he is surrounded by a mass of books such as I have never before seen assembled in one place'. Pace, Spinelli continues, had been learning Hebrew and Chaldean in order to produce a new, more textually authentic version of the Old Testament, 'in which he has found so many errors, especially in the Psalter, that it is quite amazing'.[1] Pace's Hebrew teacher was another leading English humanist scholar, Robert Wakefield, the first lecturer in the subject at the University of Cambridge. They had spent the preceding three months together at Syon working on the book of Ecclesiastes. In August of the same year, Pace was visited at Syon by the Dutch scholar John Crucius, a member of the humanist circles around William Blount, lord Mountjoy, who had been Erasmus's patron. Also in 1527, Pace engaged in debate with another regular visitor to Syon, John Fisher, bishop of Rochester and one of the leading intellectuals, theologians and politicians of the day, regarding the divine inspiration of the Septuagint (the Greek translation of the Old Testament). Thomas More, too, would make the short journey from his house in Chelsea to the Bridgettine Abbey. Another frequent visitor was the queen, Katherine of Aragon, herself a woman of significant educational accomplishment, fluent in several languages, including Latin. In 1524 she and her daughter, the Princess Mary, were rowed over the Thames from Richmond to Syon in the company of the Spanish humanist Juan Luis Vives. Vives later recalled the conversation they shared on the return journey: Katherine told him 'that she preferred moderate and steady fortune to great alternations of rough and smooth. But if she had to choose, she would elect the saddest, rather than the most flattering fortune, because in the former consolation can be found, whilst in the latter, often even sound judgment disappears.'[2]

Katherine, of course, was to get her wish, and Syon, too, would be caught up in the turbulence of the 1530s. Drawn by Syon's 'mass of books', including (as we have seen) the latest humanist editions, and also no doubt by friendships and the opportunity for academic discussion with the abbey's learned brethren, the men who visited Syon were some of the leading intellectuals of Tudor England. But among those who met there, also, were four of England's first Catholic martyrs.

The Syon brethren of this time included the confessor general John Fewterer and the priest-brothers William Bonde, Richard Reynolds and Richard Whitford. In their previous lives they had been humanist scholars, and had assembled a great library of the so-called 'new learning' that they were able to share with their humanist friends. But their own writings were of a different temper, and reflected instead their Bridgettine vocation of pastoral care and spiritual counsel. They were notable, however, for their use of the vernacular, and their ready exploitation of the medium of print.

The old idea that print and Protestantism were inevitably and exclusively associated with each other has been re-evaluated in recent years, as scholars have started to detail the range of ways in which the late-medieval Church engaged with the new technology. We have seen that Syon reacted swiftly to the arrival of printed books in England with a thorough remodelling of its library. Its first involvement in the production of printed books seems to have come towards the end of the fifteenth century, when manuscripts from its collections were used as copy text by Wynkyn de Worde, who took over William Caxton's workshop in 1495. Among them was a *Life of St Jerome* written in the first half of the century by Simon Winter, one of the early brothers, which de Worde issued in 1499, and this was followed in the next year by *A Right Profitable Treatise . . . to dispose men to be virtuously occupied in their minds and prayers* by Thomas Betson, Syon's librarian. It is not clear whether Betson had written originally with print in mind, but both works display an interest in expanding their readership, and the circulation of Bridgettine devotion, beyond the confines of the cloister.

In the 1520s and 1530s, however, Syon became a major centre for the writing of works intended for print publication. Bonde, Fewterer and Whitford were the key figures. (Reynolds, though perhaps the leading scholar of the group, so far as we know wrote nothing for publication.) Bonde's *Pilgrimage of Perfection* (1526) and *Directory of Conscience* (1527), and Fewterer's *Mirror or Glass of Christ's Passion* (1534), combined traditional forms (the book of religious instruction, meditations on the Passion) with some elements drawn from cutting-edge continental authors who had not previously been available in English. But Whitford was the best-seller. Styling himself 'the wretch of Syon', and cultivating 'a plain style, without inkhorn terms',[3] he wrote at least six original works and translated half a dozen more between 1525 and 1541. He is at home in print culture. In his preface to *The Daily Exercise and Experience of Death* (1534), Whitford explains that he first wrote the treatise 'more than 20 years ago', at the request of Abbess Elizabeth Gibbs. But demand for the work had now outstripped his capacity to keep up. 'Now of late I have been compelled, by the charitable instance and request of divers devout persons, to write it again and again. And because that writing unto me is very tedious, I thought better to put it in print'.[4] He was popular as well as prolific: many of his works ran into several editions.

Whitford's authorship was a guarantee of orthodoxy to the reader, and to the printer a guarantee of sales. Not surprisingly, then, his name got attached to other works not certainly his. So too a woodcut that appeared first in 1519 and seems to have been recognised as the Syon stamp of approval. It shows St Bridget seated at her writing desk. She

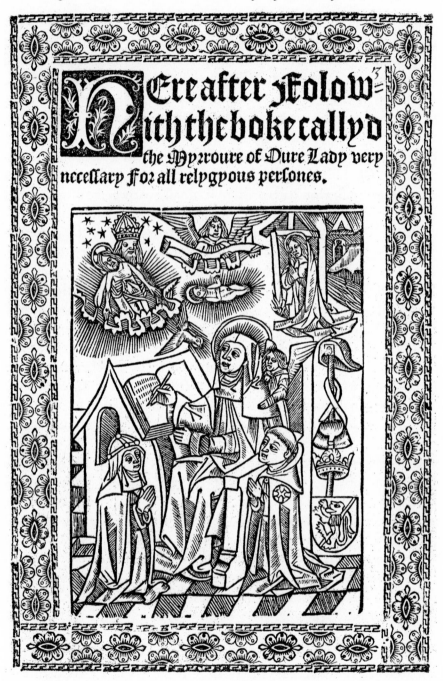

The 'Syon Bookplate'. From *The Myrroure of Oure Lady* (London: Richard Fawkes, 1530). © The British Library Board. All rights reserved. British Library shelfmark C.11.b.8.

is presumably recording her *Revelations*, since an angel is perched on her shoulder, dictating into her ear. (The pose was already familiar, as we have seen, from Syon pilgrim badges.) Above her are scenes reflecting her Christocentric devotion to the life of Jesus on earth; in the background, something that looks suspiciously like a hatstand, on which are displayed her pilgrim's hat and bag, a crown and the royal arms of Sweden; and in the foreground, a sister and brother of her order kneel at her feet. The image appeared in at least seventeen books between 1519 and 1534.

Whitford's *Work for Householders*, first published in 1530, was his most popular work; there were another six editions by 1537. It was a relatively short work, explicitly aimed at heads of secular households or 'them that have the guiding or governance of any company'. As he puts it, 'I speak unto you, good simple and devout souls, that would fain live well yourself, and also order and comfort all other unto the same'. He recommends a daily ritual that comprises morning prayer and dedication of the day to God, and an evening recollection and examination of conscience. Whitford anticipates objections from his busy, worldly readers: that such practices will waste time that could be spent working (but, he counters, it is time well spent, and will make the rest of the day go better), and that people will laugh at them for such a show of sincere piety. His response to that is worth quoting at more length, for the flavour it gives of Whitford's lively, appealing style.

> But yet some of you will say, 'Sir, this work is good for religious persons, and for such persons as be solitary and do lie alone by themselves. But we do lie 2 or sometimes 3 together, and yet in one chamber divers beds and so many in company. If we should use these things in presence of our fellows, some would laugh us to scorn and mock us.' *O Jesu bone!* O good lord Jesus! What hear I now? I dare well say there be but few persons in England but they would bide some danger or rebuke for pleasure of their king or prince, and many for their master or mistress, or their sovereigns [*superiors*], and some for their friends and fellows – and especially where great gains should grow thereby unto themselves. And for the pleasure of God our father, and of our sweet saviour Jesus our brother? Should we be abashed to take danger and bear a poor mock or scorn, that never shall wound our flesh nor yet tear our skin, for the pleasure of our peerless prince, King of kings, and Lord of all lords? Fie, for shame that any Christian should

be so cowardly. Venture upon it! Go forth withal! In 9 days (as they say) the danger shall be past.

Having advised the readers how they should comport themselves, Whitford then turns to how they should teach others. He encourages them to take responsibility for the instruction of their children, servants, and even neighbours, in the essential elements of the Christian faith: the three essential prayers, *Pater Noster* (Our Father), *Ave Maria* (Hail Mary) and *Credo* (Creed); the ten commandments, seven deadly sins, and seven works of mercy. The detailed expositions are enlivened with proverbs and anecdotes, alongside quotations from authoritative Christian writers. The work culminates in a model act of confession that readers can use in their own examination of conscience, and a brief 'potted history' of the life of Christ based around a list of keywords that is designed to help the reader commit it to memory:

> Incarnation – nativity – circumcision – epiphany – presentation – Egypt – disputation – humiliation – education – baptism – wilderness – fast – temptation – victory – election – preaching – teaching – labours – miracles – maundy – ministry – consecration – sermon – agony – betraying – taking – bishops – Pilate – Herod – Pilate again – examination – flagellation – coronation – condemnation – fatigation [*exhaustion*] – crucifixion – sepulture – resurrection – ascension – mission [*sending, sc. of the Holy Spirit*].

With its quietly confident restatement of the traditional route to salvation and the avoidance of Hell, including sacramental confession, its assumption that a summary life of Christ (and not the gospels in English) is what his readers want, its unselfconscious advocacy of devotion to the saints and of the Church fathers (and St Bridget), and careful exposition of the Latin prayers of the Church, Whitford's *Work for Householders* offers an engaging reassertion of late-medieval Catholicism. One could read it and not realise that Lutheran ideas had been streaming into England throughout the 1520s, throwing all of the foregoing traditions and assumptions into question.

But Whitford could also adopt an explicitly controversialist stance. *The Pipe or Tun of the Life of Perfection* (1532) is a lengthy commentary on and vigorous defence of the monastic or religious life. (The title alludes to an opening allegory, in which wine stored in a tun or barrel is used to represent the life of perfection, which is most securely contained within the religious life.) Whitford begins by telling us that 'This work was written years ago' and, though there is no real reason to doubt the truth of that statement, it is also a good bit of rhetoric since, in such debates, orthodoxy and antiquity regularly go together, and Whitford goes on to equate novelty with heresy: the work is 'now thought necessary to be sent forth because of newfangled persons which indeed be heretics (although they will not [*do not want to*] so be called), that do write new opinions, and do not only deprave all religions that commonly be called by that name "religion", but also do corrupt the high religion of all religions, the New Testament of Christ'. He imagines heretical (broadly, Lutheran) objections to the vowed religious life, and offers a robust, point-by-point refutation.

—·—

By 1532, when *The Pipe* was published, the monastic order was already in need of defence, but matters would worsen during the course of the 1530s.

In 1527, after eighteen years of marriage that had produced a daughter, the Princess Mary, but no living male heir, King Henry VIII had initiated manoeuvres to set aside Katherine of Aragon. Katherine had been married first to Henry's elder brother Arthur, but he had died aged fifteen within months of their marriage; Henry married her soon after. In his reading of the Bible, Henry had discovered among the incest prohibitions in Leviticus 18 the command 'Thou shalt not uncover the nakedness of thy brother's wife: because it is the nakedness of thy brother' (18: 16) and, at Leviticus 20: 21, 'He that marrieth his brother's wife, doth an unlawful thing . . . they shall be without children'. Interpreting 'without children' as 'without a son' or 'without an heir' (the Latin is *absque liberis*, 'without issue'), Henry saw an explanation for his situation: it was because he had incurred God's displeasure for an incestuous marriage that he now lacked a male heir. He also wanted to marry Anne Boleyn.

The king sought an annulment of his marriage to Katherine on the grounds that Leviticus made it illegal, and it should never have been allowed to take place. He appealed to the pope but, caught between political opposition from the emperor, Katherine's nephew Charles V, and being forced to admit the fallibility of his predecessor (and, by implication, of the papal office) in permitting the union to go ahead, Pope Clement VII resisted or prevaricated, while Henry and his ministers lobbied, took legal and theological advice, and explored all possible routes to bring what became known as 'The King's Great Matter' to a satisfactory conclusion. By 1530, the king had decided to take the pope out of the equation altogether. In 1531 he prevailed upon convocation to acknowledge him as supreme head of the Church in England 'as far as the law of Christ allowed', and during 1532 proceeded to bully the clergy into removing even that saving clause from their submission. In January 1533 Henry was secretly married to Anne Boleyn, and in May of that year his newly appointed archbishop of Canterbury, Thomas Cranmer, declared the king's marriage to Katherine of Aragon to have been invalid.

Syon Abbey was by no means insulated from this course of events. The two most prominent opponents of the royal divorce, More and Fisher, were frequent visitors, as we have seen, and Fisher later admitted to having sent his book opposing the divorce and copies of secret correspondence between himself and the king to the brethren. Richard Pace and Robert Wakefield, who learned Hebrew together at Syon in the 1520s, were both deeply enmeshed in the King's Great Matter in the years that followed. In 1532 a member of the parliament that debated the royal supremacy, Sir George Throckmorton, who was minded to oppose the king, came to Syon (perhaps at Fisher's suggestion) to ask Richard Reynolds his advice. Reynolds counselled that he should follow his conscience, whatever the cost – advice consistent with Reynolds's own behaviour later, but which Throckmorton (for the time being, at least) decided he could not follow.

The community also found itself implicated in the affair of Elizabeth Barton, the 'Holy Maid of Kent'. Barton was an obscure servant on one of the archbishop of Canterbury's manors in Kent when, in the mid-1520s, she began to have visions and to make minor prophecies. Their content was unexceptionably pious, and not dissimilar to that of other aspiring holy women of the late Middle Ages, but her reputation for holiness was sufficient for her to come to the archbishop's attention, and for her to be placed as a novice at the priory of St Sepulchre in Canterbury. Towards the end of the decade, however, her visions and prophecies turned to the matter of the king's divorce. God, she said, was highly displeased with the king. If he went ahead with the divorce and married again, 'then his majesty should not be king of this realm by the space of one month after, and in the reputation of God should not be king one day nor one hour'. He would die a villain's death, and Barton had been granted a vision of the precise place assigned him in hell.[5] Despite – or in some cases because of – the inflammatory nature of her prophecies, she found a ready audience that included prominent ecclesiastics, religious, and courtiers. In 1533 she was staying at Syon when the abbess recommended her to the marquess and marchioness of Exeter.[6] She met some of the brothers (who had their reservations about her) and, on a subsequent visit, Thomas More spoke with her in a chapel at the abbey. Surprisingly, given what she had been saying about him, Henry did not act against her until 1533 – apparently waiting until a month after his marriage to Anne Boleyn, just in case – but when he did he was relentless, confining her to the Tower, forcing a confession that her revelations were feigned, followed by a public denunciation, before she and five of her supporters were executed for treason in April 1534.

In that same month, with Thomas Cromwell now installed as his chief minister, Henry took steps to secure the new political status quo and to identify and eliminate dissent. Parliament passed the Act of Succession, which required every one of the king's subjects to swear an oath of allegiance to Henry, his lawful wife Queen Anne, and their children as legitimate heirs to the throne of England; to refuse to do so would be considered treason. Among the first to refuse the oath were Thomas More and John Fisher, who were sent to the Tower in mid-April. In May, the monks of the London charterhouse took the oath, though it took a spell in the Tower for the prior and several monks, and an armed escort for the king's commissioners, before they would comply; and when they did swear, they did so with the rider 'so far as it is lawful'. Reluctant outward compliance, rather than the outright resistance of a More or a Fisher, seems to have been the initial reaction at Syon, too. But in the summer of 1534 tensions came to the surface. Priests were expected, in their sermons, to pray for the king, Queen Anne, and their issue, and to make mention of the king's title as head of the Church in England. In the sermon he delivered on 23 August, Richard Whitford failed to do so. When it came to David Curson's turn to mention the king's title, he did so with a *mea culpa*, and on 24 August Robert Rygote similarly made it clear that he acknowledged Henry as head of the Church only under duress and on the command of his superiors, whose consciences would have to answer for what he said. Half the brothers walked out in solidarity with Rygote's act of resistance. Thomas Bedyll, who reported these goings-on to his master Thomas Cromwell a few days later, identified Whitford and another priest-brother, Richard Lache, as the 'vauntperlers' (or ringleaders) 'and heads of their faction'. He went on that he had hoped that the confessor general, John Fewterer, might be able to keep them in line, but now it is obvious that 'he can do no good with them, and that the obstinate persons be not in fear of him, but he in great fear and danger of his life, by reason of their malice, which grudge sore against him, for that he hath consented to the king's . . . title, and hath preached the same'. Bedyll says he despairs 'of their reformation by any gentle and favourable manner', and instead suggests sending spies to the brothers' sermons, so that if any of them failed to support the king's title, or walked out of the sermon of one who did, then the king's agents might arrest them, 'and bring them to prison, to the terrible example of their adherents, and to the discharging of the house of Syon of such corrupt and malicious persons'.[7]

It is painful to see the old Cambridge colleagues, and partners in Syon's printing ventures of the earlier 1530s, Whitford and Fewterer, thus at odds. (The third member of that group, William Bonde, had died in 1530.) But it fell to the other prominent Cambridge humanist among the brothers, Richard Reynolds, to take on the role of the 'terrible example'. In November 1534 parliament passed the Act of Supremacy, which recognised King Henry as 'the only supreme head on earth of the Church of England', and required every person holding ecclesiastical or other public office to swear an oath to the same effect. When the royal commissioners came to Syon to administer the oath in April 1535, Reynolds refused to swear, and was sent to the Tower. He was tried together with the priors of three charterhouses, London, Beauvale (in Nottinghamshire) and Axholme (Lincolnshire), who had also refused the oath. Cromwell led the interrogation himself. When he came to ask Reynolds why he persisted in denying the royal supremacy against the judgement of 'so many lords and bishops in parliament and the whole realm', Reynolds replied:

I had intended to imitate our lord Jesus Christ when he was questioned by Herod and not to answer. But since you compel me to clear both my own conscience and that of the bystanders, I say that if we propose to maintain opinions, by proofs, testimony, or reasons, mine will be far stronger than yours, because I have all the rest of Christendom in my favour: – I dare even say all this kingdom, although the smaller part holds with you, for I am sure the larger part is at heart of our opinion, although outwardly, partly from fear and partly from hope, they profess to be of yours.[8]

Expressing his regret that the king had been misled into error, Reynolds denied treason, but was convicted all the same, and sentenced with the Carthusians to be hanged, drawn and quartered.

The standard punishment for high treason had been devised towards the end of the thirteenth century. (The Scottish rebel William Wallace was one of the first to suffer death in this way, in 1305. It remained the statutory penalty into the nineteenth century.) Victims were first drawn or dragged to the place of execution on a wooden frame or hurdle. There they were hanged by the neck, but taken down before they lost consciousness. Their genitals were cut off, they were disembowelled, and their entrails and other internal organs burned. Finally the bodies were beheaded and chopped into four pieces, the heads and quarters being boiled to preserve them for display in prominent locations (the heads typically on London Bridge). It was a horrible way to die, but it was also importantly a spectacle. The punishment was designed to inflict as much pain and humiliation as possible on the victim, but also to inspire terror in its audience. Reynolds, the three Carthusians, and another priest, John Hale, vicar of Isleworth, who had also denied the supremacy, were executed at Tyburn, just west of London, on 4 May 1535. It was said that Henry VIII came in disguise to see the sentence carried out. Contemporaries were shocked to see the victims still dressed in their religious habits: condemned priests were normally 'degraded' (stripped of their habits and clerical status) before execution. The men were executed one by one, so that each could witness the full horror of the process before his own turn came. Reynolds was the last to suffer, and a contemporary witness noted that 'Keeping God before his eyes as he saw the gruesome murder of his companions, with a constancy and courage

Detail from 'The Martyrdom of the English Carthusian Fathers'
(and Richard Reynolds). Broadside, Rome, 1555.
British Museum 1854,1113.151. © Trustees of the British Museum.

more than heroic he preached a godly and noble sermon to the people. He never paused for a word. His voice never faltered. Nothing in his manner suggested fear or the imminence of death'.[9] Reynolds and the Carthusians were quickly recognised as martyrs. A broadsheet printed in Rome in 1555 and depicting scenes from the executions was hugely popular across Europe, and in the England of Queen Mary. A piece of the stone column from the gatehouse of Syon Abbey on which part of Reynolds's body was displayed was preserved as a relic by the Syon community. They took it with them when they left England, and carried it with them throughout their exile. It still stood in the convent chapel when the abbey closed in 2011. (It may now be seen at the church of the Blessed Sacrament in Heavitree, Exeter, near to the probable place of Reynolds's birth.) Reynolds was beatified in 1886, and canonised as one of the forty martyrs of England and Wales in 1970. Their shared feast day is 4 May.

Reynolds had been made an example of, but resistance at Syon did not suddenly evaporate. At the end of the year, Thomas Bedyll was back at the abbey, wrestling with the obdurate Whitford. 'I handled Whitford in the garden both with fair words and foul', he reports, and made various threats against him. 'But he hath a brazen forehead which shameth at nothing'.[10] Other factions, however, were more compliant. Fewterer died in 1536 and was succeeded as confessor general by John Coppinger. He had been one of the brothers who walked out of Rygote's sermon in 1534, but was now sufficiently Cromwell's man to be used to try and 'turn' other religious. He was sent two Carthusians of Beauvale, and in September 1536 wrote to Cromwell that 'since their coming to me I have shown them such reasons as I perceive they do give much credit to, so that I trust the visitors on their return will find them conformable'.[11] Even then, surveillance and intimidation continued alongside resistance, and when the laybrother Thomas Brownell interrupted a sermon to challenge the king's title, he was thrown into Newgate gaol, where he died on 21 October 1537.

Cromwell's agents seem to have concentrated their efforts on the brothers, and it is their struggles and debates that we know the most about. We have less idea what was going on in the sisters' enclosure. Such glimpses as we get are contradictory. Early in 1534 Anne Boleyn paid a visit to the nuns, but (in contrast to Katherine of Aragon, who had been a regular visitor) she received a frosty reception, initially being refused entry to their choir, and when she attempted to introduce them to evangelical ideas they listened with barely polite reluctance.[12] That August, however, Bedyll informed Cromwell that 'the abbess, and all her religious sisters, like good, wise, and faithful ladies to our sovereign lord, be well contented with the king's grace's ... title, and will be ready to declare their consents to the same, whensoever they shall be required'.[13] A year later, on the other hand, the courtier Andrew Windsor was at Syon still trying to persuade his sister, Margaret, who was prioress, and others of his kin among the nuns, to acknowledge the royal supremacy. But they refused. At the end of 1535, Bedyll tried another tack. With Confessor General Fewterer at his side he addressed

Visitation and Surrender of Syon Nunnery to the Commissioners, 1539 (oil on canvas)
Paul Falconer Poole, RA (1806-79). © Bristol Museum and Art Gallery, UK/Bridgeman Images

the nuns in the chapterhouse. The sisters were advised to give their acquiescence to the king's title as head of the Church. All in favour were to remain seated, while those against should get up and leave. Understandably enough, no-one got up, but as soon as Bedyll left one of the nuns, Agnes Smith, started to urge her sisters not to give in. Prospects for a resolution seemed as remote as ever.

Whether or not Henry had at this point formed the intention to abolish monasticism in England entirely is still debated by historians. The Act for the Dissolution of the Lesser Monasteries was passed by parliament early in 1536, and provided for the suppression of houses with an income of less than £200 a year. Houses that small were in many cases already ailing, and their long-term viability in doubt, so was this an attack on the religious orders *per se*, or simply an act of rationalisation designed to produce a leaner, fitter, monastic institution in England? And how far can the dissolution be seen as part of the programme of a committed evangelical, and how far just an opportunist expropriation of monastic lands for Henry and his cronies? There is some evidence of growing Protestant convictions to go alongside the king's impatience with elements in the Catholic establishment, but it may have been the revolt known as the Pilgrimage of Grace, which erupted in the north of England in the wake of the act, and in which the monasteries emerged as a focus for, or even a source of, sedition, that was decisive in turning Henry against the religious orders entirely.

Rather than suppress the remaining monasteries by act of parliament, Cromwell pursued a policy of piecemeal dissolution. His commissioners toured the country visiting each religious house in turn, inviting their superiors to make a voluntary surrender of the monastery into the king's hands. It was an invitation they could not refuse. The grant of a pension for life was used as an inducement for the inmates to comply, while the commissioners also looked for evidence (or rumour) of financial irregularity or sexual misconduct that could be used to blackmail a community into submission. And there was always the threat of violence. With little realistic prospect of a continuation of the monastic state, almost every house that was visited sooner or later agreed to surrender. The few exceptions were punished with exemplary harshness. The abbots of Reading, Colchester and Glastonbury were executed for treason, the latter hanged and quartered on Glastonbury Tor.

When it became clear that Syon would not respond to either threat or blandishment, however, Cromwell decided to proceed to the desired outcome on a legal technicality. The statute of *Praemunire* dated back to the fourteenth century, and forbade any subject of the English crown from appealing to or subjecting themselves to a foreign jurisdiction. It was designed in particular to set limits to papal intervention in English affairs, and as such formed part of a long struggle to define the boundaries between national and papal power, that reaches back at least as far as Thomas Becket. Convicted offenders against the statute faced the possibility of imprisonment, and the forfeiture of their lands and property. The law fell into abeyance after the end of the fourteenth century, but took on a new life during the struggles of the 1530s. On 29 May 1538, a writ of *Praemunire* was issued against John Stokesley, the bishop of London. On three occasions in 1537 and 1538 Stokesley, as diocesan bishop, had presided at the professions of brothers at Syon. The Bridgettine profession ceremony included, as it always had, an explicit acknowledgement of papal authority in the form of Martin V's confirmation of the order's rule. Specifically, Stokesley was accused of 'attributing authority to the see of Rome and to the present bishop of Rome' and performing 'various papistical rites and superstitions, such as the blessing and exorcising of vestments, cowls, mantles, etc.'. Abbess Agnes Jordan, Coppinger as confessor general, another brother and one of the nuns, were named as accessories. The bishop, recalling 'what pains I took to persuade them of Syon to renounce the bishop of Rome, and at every profession since the late statutes I have caused them to take the oath according thereto', threw himself on the king's mercy, and was pardoned.[14] But Syon would not be so fortunate. Satisfied that they now had what they needed, the authorities did not proceed against the abbey for another eighteen months. In October 1539, however, Cromwell made a note to himself 'The monastery of Syon to come by *praemunire*', and by 25 November government agents had dissolved the abbey.[15] On that date pensions were assigned to fifty-two choir sisters and four laysisters, and twelve priests and five laybrothers – that is, close to the full Bridgettine complement of eighty-five.

Despite their offence against the statute, and their earlier intransigence, members of the community were assigned generous pensions. The abbess Agnes Jordan received the very significant sum of £200 per annum, and the prioress Margaret Windsor £33 13s 4d, while the amounts allocated to ordinary choir sisters, between £6 and £8, and to the brothers (between £6 13s 4d and £15) compare favourably with the average pensions assigned elsewhere, of £5 per annum for a monk and £3 for a nun. If the accepting of pensions implies compliance, no signed deed of surrender was ever submitted, and the community took their keys and the abbey seal with them when they left. And their subsequent actions show that significant numbers of them both remained committed to the Bridgettine life, and looked forward to the day when monasticism, and the Catholic faith in all its aspects, would return to England.

Notes

1. Richard Rex, *The Theology of John Fisher* (Cambridge: Cambridge University Press, 1991), pp. 149–50.

2. Foster Watson, *Luis Vives* (Oxford: Oxford University Press, 1922), pp. 75–6.

3. *The Rule of Saynt Augustyne* (London: Wynkyn de Worde, 1525), sig. A.ii^v.

4. *Ibid.*, sig. A.i^v.

5. See her life by Diane Watt in the *Oxford Dictionary of National Biography*.

6. *Letters and Papers, Foreign and Domestic, of the Reign of Henry VIII*, ed. J. S. Brewer *et al.*, 21 vols (London: HMSO, 1862–1932), vol. 6, no. 1468.

7. Aungier, *History and Antiquities*, p.437.

8. *Letters and Papers 8*, no. 661

9. Maurice Chauncy, *The Passion and Martyrdom of the Holy English Carthusian Fathers*, ed. G. W. S. Curtis (London: SPCK, 1935), p. 97.

10. *Letters and Papers 9*, no. 986.

11. *Letters and Papers 11*, no. 487.

12. Alexandra Da Costa, *Reforming Printing: Syon Abbey's Defence of Orthodoxy 1525–1534* (Oxford: Oxford University Press, 2012), p. 115.

13. Quoted in Aungier, *History and Antiquities*, p. 437.

14. *Letters and Papers 13*(i), no. 1096.

15. *Letters and Papers 14*(ii), no. 427.

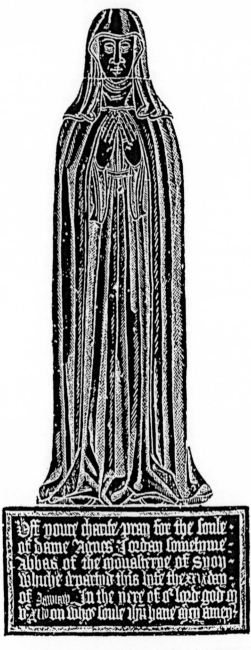

Agnes Jordan's brass at Denham.
© *The Monumental Brasses of Buckinghamshire*,
by William Lack, H. Martin Stuchfield and Philip Whittemore (1994)

4

✤ *Wanderings* ✤

ALL ACROSS ENGLAND in the 1530s religious men and women were being turned out of their monasteries. Many former monks were able to find employment as secular priests – curates or chaplains – while the rest moved into a range of other occupations. Nuns found it harder to make an independent life for themselves outside the nunnery, and most simply returned to their families. On Syon's suppression, the Fettyplace sisters, Eleanor Fettyplace and Dorothy Goodrington, went with their cousin Ursula Fettyplace, their niece Elizabeth Yate, and four other nuns to Elizabeth's father's house of Buckland, Berkshire. In their case, at least, however, the return to the family home is unlikely to have represented a meek admission of defeat. The Yate family was strongly traditional in religion. Elizabeth's uncle's house, Lyford Grange, 10 km or so from Buckland, remained a centre of dissident Roman Catholic activity well into the reign of Elizabeth: it was here (as we shall see) that Edmund Campion was captured in 1581. As for the remaining members of the community, Syon's distinctive Bridgettine constitution allowed them to come up with a novel plan for survival in the aftermath of the monastery's closure. The community divided into smaller groups, each group comprising a number of nuns (between four and eight), at least one brother to say mass and administer the sacraments for the rest of the group, and a laybrother to help with their practical needs. The nuns were chosen with an eye to sustainability: each group included at least one senior nun to provide leadership, and several of the younger members of the community, who might be expected to keep Syon's name and Bridgettine observance alive into the next generation.

Half a dozen such groups were formed and went to live in various locations around the home counties. The largest group accompanied the abbess, Agnes Jordan, to Denham in Buckinghamshire, where she took a lease on a large farmhouse called Southlands, and turned it into a miniature version of a Bridgettine monastery, with some kind of enclosure and a richly furnished chapel. The various groups must have remained in contact with each other, because there is evidence for a certain amount of movement between them. Richard Whitford joined Agnes Jordan's group in 1542, and when the prioress Margaret Windsor died in 1545 the surviving members of her group also came to Southlands. But the abbess died the following January and, with the loss of the income from her substantial pension of £200, the group was unable to continue.

At this point in Syon's story, Katherine Palmer takes centre stage. Like many of Syon's recruits, she was from a gentry family with lands in Sussex and Kent. It was a family divided by a common religion. Two of Katherine's brothers were close allies of Thomas Cromwell, one of whom, Thomas Palmer, would be executed in 1553 for his part in the scheme to put the Protestant Lady Jane Grey on the throne ahead of the Catholic Mary Tudor. Katherine Palmer had probably been a Bridgettine for less than ten years when Syon was closed down in 1539. A long-standing tradition within the community says that Palmer took a small group with her into exile in Antwerp immediately after the suppression of the abbey, where they stayed with a community of Augustinian canonesses founded by the moneyer Falco de Lampagne, and popularly known as Falcon's Cloister (in Dutch, Falconklooster). The Falcon Sisters provided the community with temporary refuge on several occasions during their later 'wanderings'. Some historians have doubted this first flight into the Low Countries, citing a lack of clear evidence for it, though perhaps that is not surprising given its necessarily clandestine nature. Palmer does seem to have been at Southlands with Abbess Jordan for some of the 1540s, but she may well have been abroad at least briefly during this time on reconaissance, because after Jordan's death, she initiated a migration to the continent. In June 1550 she arrived at the Bridgettine convent of Maria Troon (Mary's Throne) at Dendermonde in what is now Belgium, about 35 km south-west of Antwerp. Over the next few years the remnants of the various Syon groupings gradually reassembled at Dendermonde, leaving in England only the group of kinswomen who had taken refuge at the Yates's house at Buckland.

What of the community's former home of Syon in Isleworth? Un-like the majority of former monastic buildings it was not sold off to developers. As a substantial complex on the major routes by road and river into London, and situated conveniently half way between Windsor and Westminster, it was a valuable royal asset. There is no evidence that Henry VIII used it as a residence himself, but he found a range of uses for it. Catherine Howard was confined here after her condemnation during the winter of 1541–2, before being taken by boat to the Tower for her execution. Henry himself died in January 1547. His body lay in state in Whitehall for two weeks before it was taken to Windsor for burial. On that final journey a gruesome prophecy was fulfilled. At the time of the divorce Henry had been denounced from the pulpit by William Peto, a friar at Greenwich, who likened him to the biblical Ahab, whose blood, Elijah had prophesied, would be licked up by dogs (see 1 Kings 21–2). At the end of the first stage of its journey, Henry's cortege spent the night at Syon. 'At which time', according to the contemporary Nicholas Harpsfield, 'were it for the jogging and shaking of the chariot or for any other secret cause, the coffin of lead, wherein his dead corpse was put, being riven and cloven, all the pavement of the church was with the fat and the corrupt putrefied blood dropped out of the said corpse foully embrued [*stained*].'¹ The next morning, when workmen came to repair the damage, they found a dog licking up the dead king's blood.

Henry was succeeded by his nine-year-old son by Jane Seymour, Edward VI. Soon after Edward's accession the Syon estate was granted to the king's uncle, the Royal Protector Edward Seymour, duke of Somerset. After Somerset's fall from power in 1549, Syon passed to his effective successor as regent, John Dudley, president of the king's council, earl of Warwick and from 1551 duke of Northumberland. King Edward's health was never good and by the middle of 1553 he was mortally ill. In a change to his will he excluded his half-sisters Mary and Elizabeth from the succession, instead nominating his sixteen-year-old cousin Lady Jane Grey, a lineal descendant of Henry VII, and a committed Protestant, who had recently been married to Northumberland's son Guildford Dudley. (Historians debate the extent to which Northumberland influenced the king in his decision, though there is certainly no evidence that he tried to dissuade him.) Edward died on 6 July and Northumberland had Jane brought to Syon. It was here, on 9 July 1553, that she was told that she was now queen of England, before going by boat to the Tower of London, where she was publically proclaimed queen the next day. Her reign, however, if reign it can be called, famously lasted just nine days. Having proclaimed Jane queen, Northumberland failed to consolidate his position, and Mary Tudor rallied support and entered London, and was herself proclaimed queen of England on 19 July. Jane Grey, Guildford Dudley and his father Northumberland were convicted of high treason, and Northumberland was executed on 22 August.

———•———

Mary, with her husband Philip II of Spain, now set about returning England to the Catholic fold. The chief architect of the restoration would be Cardinal Reginald Pole, papal legate to England and a focus for opposition to the English reformation since the reign of Henry VIII. His mother, we recall, had lodged at Syon for several years as one of a number of aristocratic widows attracted to the abbey's environs. Exiled from England since the 1530s, Pole was in Brussels when Mary came to the throne. He did not return to England immediately, however: politicking kept him in exile for another eighteen months. Shortly before he left Brussels, in November 1554, he paid a visit to the Bridgettines at Dendermonde. While there, he granted an indulgence of forty days for all visitors to the convent of Maria Troon on the feast of St Catherine of Sweden, Bridget's daughter. But his other purpose in visiting seems to have been to discuss with the Dendermonde sisters' guests, the Syon community, the possibility of a return to England.

The restoration of the monasteries did not, however, come particularly early in Mary's project, though historians are divided over the explanation. Does it reflect a lack of commitment on the queen's part, or was it simply the legal and logistical complications involved in undoing the process of dissolution, that had seen monastery buildings and property granted away to numerous private individuals, or reassigned to other purposes? The first monastery to be restored was Westminster Abbey, to which a group of some twenty-five Benedictine monks returned on 21 November 1555. The Observant Franciscans of Greenwich followed soon afterwards, while a new foundation of Dominican friars was installed at the church of St Bartholomew in Smithfield. The project of restoring the monasteries, therefore, began in the area immediately around London, and it seems to have been a priority to restore houses belonging to those stricter orders that had been in the vanguard of the late-medieval reform movement. Even so it was another year before the Syon community, their neighbours, the Carthusians of Sheen, and the highly regarded Dominican nuns of Dartford, could return. Sheen had been sold at the dissolution, and Mary had to reacquire it, whilst the Dominicans had to be found a new site at King's Langley. The conventual buildings at Syon were at least in the Crown's possession, having been forfeited by Dudley as a result of his condemnation in 1553. But they no longer looked like a monastery. Protector Somerset had made substantial alterations to both the buildings and the grounds, to turn them into a residence fit for his (not inconsiderable) aspirations. He laid out an Italianate botanical garden designed by the renowned herbalist William Turner, which apparently included the first Mulberry trees planted in England, and the house impressed the Venetian ambassador as 'one of the most beautiful palaces in this neighbourhood'.[2] Two sides of the convent had been 'decayed, and pulled down' as part of the process and had to be rebuilt.[3] It is not even clear that there was still a church on the site.

It was on 16 November 1556 that religious first returned to Syon and Sheen, in the presence of Cardinal Pole. At Syon the first party consisted of those who had remained in England at Buckland; they were joined by Katherine Palmer and the group from Dendermonde a little later, and Syon was formally restored by Pole in the pope's name on 1 March 1557. The charter of restoration begins by recalling how 'in the time of that most deadly schism which lately flourished in this kingdom, the religious men and women were expelled from it, without doubt illegally, the house dissolved *de facto*, and with all its property transferred into the royal treasury, and its church and domestic buildings put to profane uses'. Now, however, noting Philip and Mary's desire 'that what had been overthrown and had fallen into ruin in that most disastrous time should be restored', Pole declares in the pope's name: '[we] restore and reinstate the said house of Syon to its former religious state and we set up and establish this house as a monastery under the same title of the Holy Saviour, the Holy Virgin Mary and St Bridget of Syon which it had before the dissolution'. The charter appoints Katherine Palmer as abbess and John Green as confessor general. The following month, Queen Mary granted to the abbess and community the site of

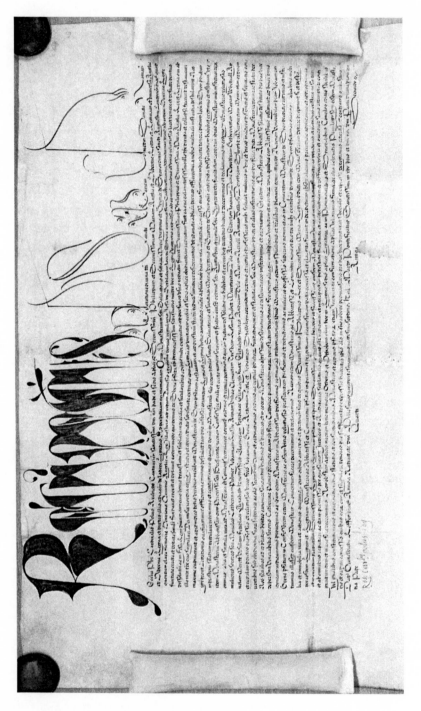

The deed of restoration, signed by Cardinal Pole.
Exeter University Library MS 389/4120.

the monastery and its precincts and the church and chapel of Isleworth. On 1 August 1557 the community of nineteen sisters and three brothers was re-enclosed by the bishop of London, Edmund Bonner. Queen Mary made further grants early in 1558, and in the will she made in April 1558 specially remembered Syon and Sheen, leaving each of them £500 'for a further increase of their living, and to the intent that the said religious persons may be the more able to re-edify some part of their necessary houses that were so subverted and defaced, and furnish themselves with ornaments and other things meet for God's service', and granting them additional endowments to a total of £100 each.[4]

There were encouraging signs of vocations to the newly restored monastery. A place was agreed for Margaret Clement, grand-daughter of Thomas More, though in the event she decided to join the Ursulines at Louvain. In 1558 a niece of Cardinal Pole was 'already with the nuns of Syon, and determined on taking the vows and living with them entirely'.[5] But there were also significant losses. Eighteen hard years had passed since the community left Isleworth, and the community had aged. Three of the sisters named in the deed of restoration died before they could be re-enclosed by the bishop of London, and John Green, whom Pole had nominated as confessor general, was too ill to attend the ceremony. Two more nuns died in 1557, and in the second half of 1558 another three succumbed to an influenza epidemic that hit the London area.

From this the community might have recovered, but the same epidemic also took Mary Tudor and Reginald Pole: queen and cardinal died on the same day, 17 November 1558. The accession of Elizabeth was quickly followed by a complete reversal of her sister's religious policy. On the opening day of business in her first parliament (30 January 1559) the recently restored monasteries were returned to the ownership of the Crown. Soon afterwards were passed a new Act of Supremacy, declaring the queen to be 'supreme governor' of the Church in England, and requiring anyone in public office to take an oath to the same effect, and the Act of Uniformity, reinstating the English services of the Book of Common Prayer. Syon and the other religious communities prepared to leave once again. Together with their neighbours from Sheen and the Dominican nuns of Dartford, the community secured the protection of the count of Feria, Gómez Suárez de Figueroa. He

Nouembris

b·13· Briai epi ⁊ conf

d·14· Machuti epi ⁊ conf
Margareta Russell. Sor. 1849

c· 16 Edmūdi cant' archi'.

c·19· Trāsl' sā erkenwaldi
Katina Clynton S⁴: 1843 ·
·2· Elizab; langthorn S⁴: 1986·

F·17· hugonis epi ⁊ cōf
Regina Maria que re
stauraūit monasterium
et religionē nrām post
schisma et fuit noua funda
trix et restauratrix coꝛd'.

Eodem die obijt Regi
naldus Polus Cardinal
et legat' a latere, q et recō
siliauit totū regnū nrm An
glie ad vnitatē cclie catho
lice, et cōstituit noua mor
parcōem de religiosis psonꝰ
que supstites fueriūt prius,
ante dissolucōem ptinentibꝰ
ad istū nrm monasteriū.
·1558·

The deaths of Queen Mary and Cardinal Pole.
The Syon Martiloge, British Library, Add. MS 22285, fol. 63v.

had been Philip II's chief representative at the court of Queen Mary during the king's frequent absences from England. Shortly after Mary's death he had married Jane Dormer, a close confidante of the queen, and a woman of impeccable Catholic credentials: her grandmother's brother was the Carthusian martyr Sebastian Newdigate. The count and countess of Feria left England in early summer 1559 and, by special licence from Queen Elizabeth, were permitted to take with them a number of Catholics into exile, including the members of the three religious communities. And so, by the beginning of August 1559, after a restoration that had lasted barely two-and-a-half years, Katherine Palmer and her group of Bridgettines were back at the abbey of Maria Troon in Dendermonde.

———•———

It must have seemed a natural place to take refuge from the turbulence of the English Reformation. The Low Countries were close neighbours, long-standing allies and trading partners, some of the Syon community already had connections there, and they were part of the Hapsburg Empire ruled by the late queen's husband, Philip II of Spain. But the next twenty years turned into anything but a period of peaceful respite.

The arrangement at Maria Troon was probably always intended to be only temporary. At what point the Syon community resigned themselves to a lengthy exile is impossible to know, but when, in 1561, they were joined by a further nine sisters from England – women who had initially chosen not to make the journey to the continent, but now repented their decision – they must have known it was time to look for their own premises. Abbess Katherine Palmer petitioned the pope for his support, and appealed to the Spanish regent in the Low Countries, Margaret of Parma, for her assistance in finding a suitable site. Through the latter's intercession, the community was granted a pension of 1200 florins a year from Philip II. The pope was slower to respond. In fact, Abbess Palmer did not receive his reply until 1565, by which time its immediate relevance to the move from Dendermonde had passed. But the rescript of Pope Pius IV, dated 8 May 1564, was more wide-ranging than that, and was cherished as an essential document during Syon's years of wandering. (Indeed it remains with their archive to this day.) In it, the pope explicitly acknowledged the present community as 'the lawful corporate college and monastery of Syon as it was aforetime

The arrival in Flanders, from *History of the Peregrinations of the Syon Nuns*, 1620s.
© His Grace The Duke of Norfolk, Arundel Castle/Bridgeman Images.

in England; a fixed establishment, called by its name and known as a permanent foundation'.[6] In other words, this was official recognition of the continuity of Syon's existence since before Henry VIII's dissolution.

The move away from Dendermonde was made late in 1563, when the community purchased the empty convent of Bethany at Haamstede near Zierikzee on the island of Schouwen. The Dartford nuns were settled not far away, at Leliendael; perhaps they alerted the community to the property's availability. Unfortunately, however, the new site was not a success. The environment was marshy (Haamstede today is 1 m above sea level) and unhealthy, and the community lost five sisters and two brothers between 1565 and 1567. In August 1567, Katherine Palmer was seeking to have the pope 'authorise their migration from the islands to which for lack of other retreat they have been relegated, where the necessaries of life are hardly to be had and the air is unwholesome, to some more suitable residence, if they should be able to find one'.[7]

By the following January they had moved to Mishagen in the countryside near Eeckeren, outside Antwerp, where they were able to purchase convent buildings from a community of Augustinian canonesses who were relocating to Utrecht. Syon's representative in the negotiations was Nicholas Sander. He was a leading figure among the English exiles in Louvain and the most prominent and outspoken of Catholic activists during the 1570s. He died in Ireland, where he was fomenting holy war against Queen Elizabeth, in 1581. Two of his sisters, Margaret and Elizabeth (whom we shall meet again later in the chapter), were among the sixteen nuns and six brothers who made up the Syon community in 1569.

At Mishagen the climate may have been healthier, but there were new dangers. Political and religious tensions had been rising throughout the later 1560s, and in 1568 the revolt of the Protestant William of Orange against Hapsburg rule initiated the conflict that would become known as the Eighty Years War, and which eventually issued in Dutch independence from Spain. Antwerp in these years was a hotbed of radical Calvinism, and the isolated convent was a dangerous place for a small group of alien religious. In 1571 they fled Mishagen for the relative security of the Falcon sisters of Antwerp, until they could find a place of greater safety. Looking back at this episode from Lisbon, around the year 1600, they remembered it as a lucky escape: 'certain heretics had many times endeavoured to break open the doors of the monastery and

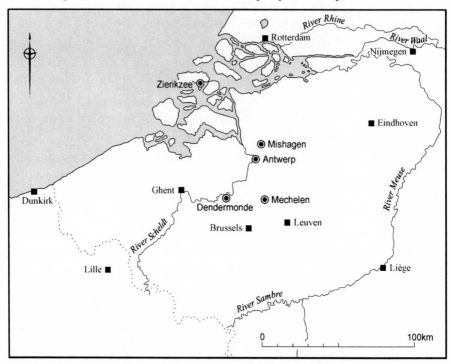

The 'wanderings' of Syon in the Low Countries. © Jane Read.

to climb their walls by night, so as those poor religious sisters stood in manifest peril of their lives and honour, and they had scarce left the house ten hours when the heretics came with carts, horses, and other preparations to carry them and their goods away'.[8]

From Antwerp they went to Mechelen, about 25 km distant, where there was a substantial community of English Catholic emigrés around the exiled Marian courtier Sir Francis Englefield, an old friend of the community. (He had paid for the rebuilding works at the original Syon in Isleworth to ready the convent for its reoccupation in the 1550s.) Around the end of 1572 Englefield found them a large townhouse with land and outbuildings, suitable for conversion to a monastery. The Syon community's life in Mechelen grew more difficult from 1575, however, when Englefield and the other English dissidents were expelled from the town, cutting off much of their access to moral and financial support. There was a further blow the following year. The sacking of Antwerp by Spanish troops in November 1576 known as the 'Spanish

Fury' sparked off anti-Catholic violence in the surrounding area. In Mechelen, a rumour was put about that weapons were being concealed in English monasteries. On 8 November 'the English convent' (as Syon was known) was attacked by rioters. A witness testified that, at about 9 pm, he heard a commotion at the convent and went to investigate. 'Curious to see what was on foot, he followed the crowd into the house and saw several citizens attempting to force the door which led into the nuns' enclosure. He begged them to desist and urged the Father to open this door and the other doors to avoid any violence. But at that moment the door was opened from within and there stood all the sisters with the aged Abbess at their head. The mob rushed past them and down into the cellar. . . . The mob ran all over the convent and searched every chest and cupboard.'[9] The abbey survived this ordeal, but its abbess did not. Katherine Palmer died on 19 December, and was succeeded by Bridget Rooke.

By 1578 the situation had become desperate. To extreme poverty and hunger was added imminent danger of attack from militant Protestants. The ecclesiastical authorities advised all nuns to leave their convents and withdraw to places of safety until the situation had become calmer. One community failed to comply and was overrun: 'Upon the fury of the "holy evangelicals" invading', it was reported, 'they stripped them stark naked, leading them by force up and down thus in their camps.'[10] At Syon, it was decided to send ten or so of the younger sisters – perhaps half the community – back to their families in England to collect alms and to lie low until it was safe to return. Disguised as Dutch women they travelled singly or in small groups, intending to meet up at a Catholic safe-house in Fulham, near London. A group of five sisters was arrested on landing at Dover, while three more were taken at Colchester. At least some of these seem afterwards to have been released and to have stayed at the home of Sir Francis Yate at Lyford Grange in Berkshire. Of those who got through unmolested, Anne Stapleton was ill when she arrived, and died before the year was out. Mary Champney spent time with the sisters at Lyford Grange, but in the spring of 1580 she was suffering with an advanced consumptive illness, and she died at the end of April. A piously inspirational account of her life and exemplary death was written for circulation among England's beleaguered Catholic community. A third Bridgettine lived to tell her own tale. We have already encountered Elizabeth Sander, sister of the firebrand Nicholas Sander, at Mishagen. Now she left the safe-house in Fulham at first for Lyford Grange, and from there went to her sister's at Alton in Hampshire. Here she began to distribute copies of Edmund Campion's 'Challenge to the Privy Council', popularly known as 'Campion's Brag'. She was arrested and imprisoned at Winchester, where the notoriety of her brother militated against any chance of release. She remained in prison until 1583, when she received a letter from Abbess Rooke bidding her return to the convent, which was now more securely settled in Rouen. She escaped from prison several times (on one occasion escaping Winchester Castle by climbing down a rope let over the castle wall) before being smuggled out of England on a false passport, reaching Rouen in 1587 and rejoining the Syon community after an absence of almost ten years.

Elizabeth Sander's story shows the extent to which Syon was enmeshed in the developing networks of English recusants both abroad and at home. The connections were inevitable: the same families who were sending their daughters to Syon were also sending sons to the English colleges, and into the Jesuits. Elizabeth's brother the belligerent Nicholas Sander was somewhat out on a limb. The mainstream of the English Catholic exiles was represented by William Allen (later Cardinal Allen), founder of the English colleges at Douai (1568) and Rome (1579), and the charismatic Jesuits Robert Persons (or Parsons) and Edmund Campion. They crossed from the continent in 1580 for the high-profile launch of Jesuit involvement in the mission for the re-conversion of England. They remained at large until summer 1581. Campion was arrested in July at Sir Francis Yates's Lyford Grange, to which he had gone, it was said, against Persons's better judgement, expressly to meet the exiled Bridgettines who were staying there. Arrested with him were two of the Syon nuns, Juliana Harman and Catherine Kingsmill. They were imprisoned at Reading, and probably died there. Campion, of course, was tried and executed for treason on 1 December, the first martyr of the 'English mission'.

Meanwhile, on 9 April 1580 Mechelen had fallen to a combined force of Dutch and English soldiers under the command of Colonel John Norris. The city was sacked in a frenzy of violence and looting that has gone down as the 'English Fury'. In the midst of it all, the Syon community was preserved by a number of English officers who – whether through simple pity, or the claims of national solidarity over confessional hostility – secured their safe conduct out of the city. They were taken, probably by water, to Antwerp. Before leaving the Low Countries for good, they made arrangements for the sale of their old convent at Mishagen, and then took passage for Rouen. Their baggage – two large and two small cases, a barrel full of books, five crates of unbound books, and a large package of pictures – was sent ahead on 17 May, and the community followed soon afterwards. Despite an encounter with English pirates they arrived safely in Rouen around the middle of July, and rented a secular house in the city.

Rouen was the administrative capital of Normandy, situated on the Seine about half way between Paris and the Channel, a busy port for ocean-going trade as well as a major centre for the manufacture of cloth. To the Syon community it must have seemed a place mercifully free from doctrinal strife, even if that calm was the legacy of a violent recent past. The long but intermittent conflict known as the French Wars of Religion had erupted in Paris in August 1572 in the so-called St Bartholomew's day massacres. Thousands of Protestants (or Huguenots, as they were known in France) were killed in the capital and in copycat attacks in a number of provincial centres, including Rouen. Protestants were a small and quiet minority in the city during these years. Rouen was also a growing centre for English Catholic exiles and oppostion to Elizabeth more generally. The archbishop of Rouen's vicar general was the exiled bishop of Ross, John Lesley, a close associate of Mary, queen of Scots, and an inveterate intriguer. George Gilbert, a prominent Catholic activist who had met Mary Champney in London in 1580 and promised his assistance, visited the Syon community here in 1581 and made them a life-saving gift of 250 gold pieces. When Robert Persons withdrew from England following Campion's arrest, he came to Rouen, where he printed his account of Campion's martyrdom, *De Persecutione Anglicana* ('The English Persecution'), ready for copies to be smuggled into England. On a subsequent visit he was said to have celebrated mass in Syon's abbey church.

But the most lastingly significant connection the community formed in these years was with Seth Foster.

Seth Foster, confessor general 1584–1628.
Photograph by Eric Thompson, from a painting now at Oscott College.
Sr Anne Smyth, personal collection.

Seth Foster (also known as Joseph) was born in Yorkshire in the mid-1550s, was educated at the English College in Rome, where he was ordained priest, taught for a year at the English seminary at Rheims, and early in 1584 set off to join the 'English mission', the underground Catholic ministry pioneered by Campion and Persons. En route from

Paris, he broke his journey at Rouen and there encountered the Syon community. He found the sisters facing a crisis. Although (as we have seen) the nuns had received a steady supply of postulants, the community had found it harder to recruit brethren, and now only a single priest remained, the aged John Johnson. The abbess and convent begged Foster to stay and, having secured permission from his superiors for this change of plan, he agreed, joined the community in March 1584, and in August of the same year was professed a Bridgettine and immediately elected as the twelfth confessor general. Foster is a key figure in the history of Syon over the next forty years and more, guiding the community through the turbulent politics of their time in France and their move to the relative security of Lisbon. In our main narrative source for this period, indeed, he is the leading figure, eclipsing the abbess – though this may be in part because of particular biases in that source. *The Wanderings of Syon* is an unashamed panegyric to Foster, whom it seems to see as a candidate for sainthood. The work, it should also be noted, dates from the community's time in Lisbon, and looks back on events through the prism of the Council of Trent, with its tendency to subordinate female religious to male confessors. (This we shall consider further in the next chapter.) Foster used his connections with the English colleges to recruit a number of priests to the order, so that by 1587 there were six brothers, the most there had been at any time during Syon's exile. He also organised a move to new rented premises in a house known as 'The Three Mallets'. Around this time, too, Sr Elizabeth Sander and (according to her information) a number of other nuns who had been imprisoned in England returned to the abbey.

Although at Syon the health of the institution was reviving, Rouen in the second half of the 1580s had fallen on hard times. The harvest failed in 1585 and again in 1586. Renewed activity by English pirates in the Channel had imposed a virtual blockade on the city, hampering imports of grain as well as disrupting trade. In 1587 an English sea captain returned from Rouen with a grim description of the hardships there: 'They die in every street and at every gate, morning and evening, by 8 or 12 in a place, so that the like hath not been heard of. And the poor doth not only die so in the street, but the rich also in their beds by 10 or 12 in a day'.[11] In the same year Abbess Rooke sent a petition or 'Supplication' to England, signed by all twenty-four sisters and six brothers, recounting that they 'do almost despair of their longer abode together and therewith of the continuing and preserving of their religion and order, wherein hitherto they have served together most religiously', and requesting aid from 'all charitable and well disposed Catholics' in order that this community, that has 'hitherto in manifold peril and with great labour endeavoured to continue their holy religion in banishment and a strange country; which also is the only religious convent remaining of our country', might continue.[12] At the same time, two of the brothers, John Marsh and John Vivian, were despatched to Spain to request payment of the arrears of the abbey's pension from Philip II, and to seek further alms from the court there. On their way back to Rouen they were captured by corsairs at La Rochelle, and handed over to an English pirate who transported them to England. One of their companions described the hardships of the passage: 'Our cheer was sour beans and stinking water ... and without any bread 8 weeks together and truly Sir it is somewhat loathsome to tell, 10 thousand companions with six legs'.[13] They were taken to London, where they were imprisoned at the Marshalsea, expecting the worst. Seth Foster, however, procured the intervention of the French ambassador and at length Marsh and Vivian were released and returned to Rouen. They brought with them David Kemp, a priest who had been captured at the same time and had been inspired to join the community.

The incident is an example of how Foster's connections enabled him to secure the community's future in the short term. But his involvement in the complex factional politics that characterised the final phases of the French wars of religion would eventually lead to Syon's departure from Rouen. In the summer of 1584 the younger brother and heir apparent of the childless King Henri III had died, leaving as the next in line to the French throne the Huguenot, Henri of Navarre. In response the various Catholic interests allied themselves together into a confederation that became known as the Catholic League. Its leader was Henri, duc de Guise, but it was bankrolled by, and later received military support from, Philip II of Spain. These were the protagonists for the final conflict of the wars of religion, known as 'The War of the Three Henrys'. Initially the king was swayed by the League to attempt to suppress Protestantism in France, but later he would ally with the Protestant Navarre against the pro-Spanish League. Alliances shifted rapidly, as plot was followed by counter-plot. In December 1588 the king had the duc de Guise assassinated, but in the following August he in turn was killed by a supporter of the League. Henri of Navarre was now nominally king of France, but he had to recapture much of the northern portion of the kingdom from forces loyal to the League. Rouen was one of its strongholds, and in August Navarre made his first attempt on the city. Syon afforded a good vantage point to see the fighting, and Sr Elizabeth Sander sent Francis Englefield a description of the battle. Navarre 'besieged the town upon our side, where we might see both sides fight. At his first mounting the hill before the town with his horsemen I and the whole company did see one of our great pieces strike down ten horsemen in the troop where Navarre was himself'. Sander leaves little doubt where her sympathies lie, adding 'I would it had hit him alone for those ten'.[14]

Navarre withdrew to wait for reinforcements from various quarters, including England. In the mean time, Foster was involving Syon ever more closely with the League. He secured new premises for the community by a direct appeal to the duc de Mayenne, its new leader, who granted him, early in 1590, a substantial townhouse left vacant by a Huguenot who had fled the city. He was able to procure stone to build a church, and 'in this house he also caused to be built a large and handsome dormitory for the sisters, with several convenient partitions or cells, and windows on both sides. And in the church he also built a large high choir, whereby they were well accommodated both in their church and dormitory, much better than they had ever been before in their banishment'.[15] In late November 1591, Navarre returned to Rouen and besieged the city. The convent laid in supplies for six months, and our main narrative source, the *Wanderings of Syon* (with a certain lack of charity), celebrates their foresight: 'By this prudent forecast it came to pass that whilst others died of hunger in the streets, while the rich became poor and the poor were without refuge, and while other cloisters that were well endowed sent their religious to their own parents through want, we saw the words of David fulfilled, . . . "the rich wanted and were hungry, but those that sought God wanted nothing" [Ps. 34: 10] . . . : for as at other times we never had, nor could have great abundance, we never felt less want than at this time, our Lord's holy name be magnified for it.'[16]

The siege was lifted after five months, in April 1592, with the arrival of Spanish forces. Prospects for a decisive resolution of the conflict seemed distant, but the following year Navarre broke the stalemate with the surprise announcement of his conversion to Roman Catholicism. Having been received into the Church in July 1593, he was recognised as king of all France, and crowned at Chartres on 17 February 1594 as Henri IV. He entered Paris on 22 March, and on the 30th of the same month, with the Catholic League outflanked, Rouen acknowledged Henri as king. Seth Foster had pinned Syon's fortunes comprehensively to those of the League, so that it now felt inevitable that the community would have to quit Rouen. The only question was whether to go by land with the Spanish army back into Flanders, or by sea to Spain. Despite the hardships of the journey, and the dangers they foresaw from hostile vessels and pirates, they chose Spain. Unable to face a return to the war zone of the Low Countries, they also considered that going by sea was 'much better, cheaper, and with less toil for women' than by land, and that on such a journey 'we might at least convey the best of our church furniture, books, movables and all our relics.'[17]

The *Wanderings* describe much sadness in Rouen at the community's departure. Wellwishers besieged the convent, protesting 'You have a fair house and church, and are well beloved, why will you go?' To which Foster answered, 'We left a better house, a better church and friends in England, viz., Old Syon in England, a royal foundation, we came not to France to seek those commodities, but to serve God in the Catholic Faith and Church, and live and die in obedience to the Church of Rome; to conclude, we neither sought England, France, nor Earth, but Heaven, which is all we now pretend to, and yourselves, and all other good Catholics are bound to do the same.'[18] On 8 April 1594, Good Friday, the community of twenty-two sisters and eight brothers sailed up the Seine for Newhaven. They were detained there for almost a month by obstructive officials and difficulties in procuring a ship, before they finally embarked on 5 May and, after two weeks' voyage, and a narrow brush with a group of English men of war, they arrived at Lisbon on 20 May, at about two o'clock in the afternoon.

Some years later, from the relative peace and security of Lisbon, the community looked back on the years of wandering endured by 'this poor, little, destitute, fleeting bark of Syon'. Since leaving England for the second time, they had spent thirty-five years 'in banishment, exiled from all comforts and conveniences, and as it were besieged with continual poverty, want of language, loss of country and kindred and almost all human help and remedy'. A comparison with the exodus of the Israelites suggests itself readily enough to the community of Syon, and it is not one that belittles the hardship of their own experiences, for

> we had not only one sea; and that but once to pass over (as the Children of Israel had) but different seas, and divers times, in the face of our enemies who with open mouth lay gaping to devour us. Neither had we so many hundred thousand armed men, with Captains and Generals daily guarding us and marching by our sides to give battle to any who should stop or injure us: on the contrary we were but a few poor orphans, friendless and harmless women, armed only with our books and beads, and having only one or two Fathers among us for our Spiritual comfort in so many extreme dangers.[19]

Notes

[1.] Nicholas Harpsfield, *A Treatise on the Pretended Divorce between Henry VIII and Catharine of Aragon*, ed. Nicholas Pocock, Camden Society n.s. 21 (1878), p. 203.

[2.] *Calendar of State Papers Relating To English Affairs in the Archives of Venice. Volume 6: 1555–1558*, ed. Rawdon Brown (London: HMSO, 1877), ii.704.

[3.] *The Wanderings of Syon*, ch. 67. For full details of this important source, see the Suggestions for Further Reading.

[4.] http://tudorhistory.org/primary/will.html.

[5.] *State Papers Venice, Volume 6*, iii.1287.

[6.] Exeter University Library 95/5, p. 213.

[7.] Exeter University Library 95/5, p. 223.

8. 'A Preface, Written by Father Robert Persons S.J., to the History of the Wanderings of Syon. From a Manuscript Preserved at Syon Abbey, Chudleigh', in Adam Hamilton, *The Angel of Syon* (Edinburgh: Sands & Co., 1905), pp. 107–8.

9. Exeter University Library 95/6, p. 103.

10. Ann M. Hutchison, 'The Life and Good End of Sister Marie', *Birgittiana* 13 (2002), 3–89, p. 60.

11. Quoted Philip Benedict, *Rouen during the Wars of Religion* (Cambridge: Cambridge University Press, 1981), p. 173.

12. Printed by Adam Hamilton in *Poor Soul's Friend* 1905–6, p. 325.

13. Letter of David Kemp to Francis Englefield, transcribed Exeter University Library 95/19, p. 231.

14. Exeter University Library 95/8, p. 303.

15. *Wanderings*, ch. 11.

16. *Ibid.*, ch. 12.

17. *Ibid.*, ch. 47.

18. *Ibid.*, ch. 51.

19. *Ibid.*, ch. 1.

5

✣ *Lisbon* ✣

In many ways, the choice of Lisbon was a good one. Since 1580, when the royal line of the House of Aviz had failed, Portugal had been ruled, in a federal arrangement known as the Iberian Union, by Syon's long-time patron, Philip II of Spain. The country was untainted by Protestant heresy or confessional conflict. Here in Europe's western-most city the traumas of the last half century would be, quite literally, half a continent away.

Moreover, England and Portugal had been allies since the fourteenth century and, though the two nations were now at odds in the matter of religion, there remained a substantial English community in the Portuguese capital. More properly, there were several English-speaking communities. There was a significant number of English merchants, reflecting Lisbon's importance as a trading centre, originally for the im-port of goods from India, and now increasingly from the New World. There was, too, a community of English Catholic emigrés, both exiled priests and members of recusant families. The Jesuit, Robert Persons, had only recently left the city. He had been in Spain since 1588, and had founded seminaries at Valladolid and Seville. He was in Lisbon in 1591–2, laying the groundwork for a residence for English Jesuit priests in the city, which opened in 1594, the year Syon arrived. (The residence would in 1622 be superseded by the English College for the training of secular priests for the English mission.) There was already a seminary for Irish priests, founded a few years earlier, in 1590, and in 1639 they would be joined by a community of Irish Dominican sisters at the convent of Bom Sucesso ('Our Lady of Good Success') at Belém, just to the west of Lisbon at the entrance to the Tagus estuary.

And yet there was some irony in the timing of Syon's departure from Rouen. Just as they were leaving, the first wave of English monastic foundations was arriving on mainland Europe. A Benedictine convent

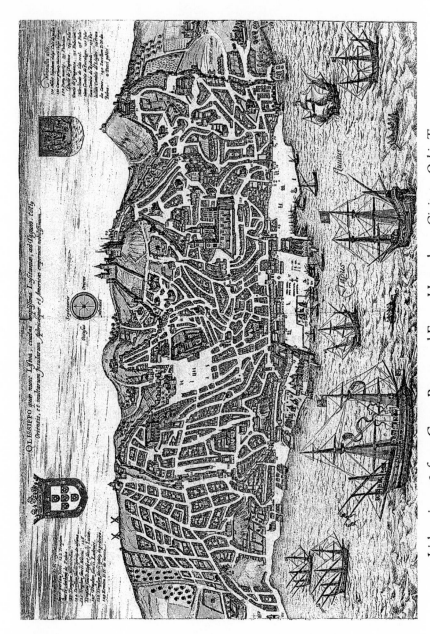

Lisbon in 1598, from Georg Braun and Franz Hogenberg, *Civitates Orbis Terrarum* (Cologne: P. Gallaeum, 1572–1617). Wikimedia Commons.

for Englishwomen was founded at Brussels in 1598; just over the French border the first continental foundation for English Benedictine monks was established at Douai Abbey in 1605. By the end of the century no fewer than twenty-one new convents for English nuns had been founded in continental Europe, and all of them could be found in a relatively small corner of northern France and Flanders, where they could benefit from regular communication and mutual support in matters both practical and spiritual. Syon's location some 2000 km to the south-west left it – not for the first (or last) time in its history – in isolation. What is more, soon after 1600 there began a revival of the Bridgettine order in the Netherlands, emanating from Syon's former hosts at Dendermonde, the convent of Maria Troon. Medieval foundations that had almost died out were restored and reinvigorated, while there were numerous new foundations of a new breed of single-sex Bridgettine monasteries, some for women only, some for men.

Still, Lisbon was welcoming. Robert Persons, who (as we have seen) had known the Syon community in Rouen and was a personal friend of the confessor general, Seth Foster, had written letters of introduction to the archbishop of Lisbon and the civic authorities to smooth their reception. King Philip sent 800 ducats, being the amount of their pension currently due, and with it they were able to pay off the master of the ship that had brought them from France. The city fathers provided an allowance of five ducats a day, and arranged for them to be lodged for the time being with the Franciscan nuns of Esperança in Mocambo (now known as Madragoa), a predominantly African district outside the western gates of the city. By the end of the year Philip had augmented their five ducats a day with an annual grant of seven hundred crowns for the next six years. And so, the community reflected, 'the weather-beaten bark of Syon was anchored in a Catholic country and better secured than it had ever been in our banishment', such that 'we expected sure peace and ease the rest of our lives, and that we had left all our troubles and vexations behind us'.[1]

———•———

Needless to say, things were not so simple. Having spent some seventy years being harassed and pursued by Protestants of various hues, it was Syon's lot now to find itself on the wrong side of the Catholic authorities. Among the group that had come from Rouen was a novice, Dorothy Shelly. By spring 1595 she was ready to make her formal profession. The rule specified that the ceremony should be performed by the diocesan bishop, and so the archbishop of Lisbon, Miguel de Castro, was contacted and a date agreed: the ceremony would take place on 28 March. But when the day came, and the guests were assembled, the archbishop sent his apologies and failed to appear. When pressed for an explanation he gave a number of reasons for his reluctance: the convent and the Bridgettine order were unknown to him; the profession rite was not included in the Roman pontifical nor concordant with the Council of Trent; in such documents as he had been sent the abbey's diocesan was identified specifically as the bishop of London; he had no proof that they had really been in Rouen, or the other places claimed, and that they were not English spies. A year of negotiations ensued, in which numerous documents were exhibited and testimony taken from witnesses and supporters. The confessor general, Seth Foster, is said to have travelled the 600 km to Madrid on foot, in order to present the abbey's case to Philip II in person. Sir Francis Englefield, who had known the community in England and the Low Countries, and who was now living among the English Catholic exiles in Spain, gave evidence; and Robert Persons wrote from Rome. In the end, to break the deadlock, the community petitioned the Holy See, and in response, by a brief of 1596, Pope Clement VIII ratified the order and took Syon directly under papal protection. In future they would answer not to the archbishop of Lisbon, but to the papal representative in Portugal, the apostolic collector, who was also based in the city.[2]

The abbey's immediate future had been secured, but the question of the conformity of its legislation and practices with the Council of Trent had been raised. The Council had met in twenty-five sessions between 1545 and 1563, and addressed not only the doctrinal and political challenges posed by Protestantism, but also the positive reform of the Roman Catholic Church and its institutions. The decisions of the Council were, however, not implemented immediately or uniformly across Europe. In France, the dogmatic decrees, reaffirming Catholic doctrine in the face of Protestant heresy, had been published in 1581, but the full range of the Council's disciplinary decrees was not ratified there until 1595, after the Syon community had left. The final session of the

Council had turned to the matter of the reform of the religious orders, and its decrees had been supplemented subsequently by a number of further rulings and declarations. A rolling programme of reforming the religious orders in accordance with the Tridentine decrees was set in train, and by the end of the sixteenth century was making its effects felt across Europe.

For religious women, the key consequences of Trent were twofold. There was, first, a renewed emphasis on strict enclosure; and secondly, the authority of nuns and their abbesses was firmly subjugated to that of their male superiors, such as the diocesan bishop or confessor. While the first of these represented no great challenge to a Bridgettine community like Syon, the second was harder to reconcile with Bridget's vision for her order. Responsibility for bringing Syon into line with Tridentine expectations was entrusted by Pope Clement VIII to the collector for Portugal, Fabrizio Caracciolo. He deputed the work of revising the abbey's constitutional documents to Emmanuell Coelho, a doctor of divinity and legal advisor to the Inquisition in Lisbon. New versions of the rule and constitutions were drawn up, formally accepted by Seth Foster as confessor general, and signed by the abbess Elizabeth Preston and each member of the community, before being approved and given force of law by Caracciolo on 19 December 1607.

Foster's leading role in the process reflects a new emphasis on the confessor general in the revised documents. As 'conservator of the order' he was now answerable for all aspects of the community's observance; he, more than the abbess, was to be the 'public face' of the community, and he would play a much more significant role in the approval and profession of novices; while the abbess was still the head of the abbey, she was now expected to consult with the confessor general on many important decisions. From what we have seen of his character, it is doubtful whether Foster balked at the greater prominence the new legislation afforded him. The abbess's position was also weakened by a revision which saw her elected only for a three-year term; hitherto, abbesses had been appointed for life. (While this change accorded with a general move towards triennial elections brought in by a papal bull of 1583, it is worth noting that confessor general continued as a lifetime appointment.)

Vere libera sum.

Nihilminus, sed feruens amor christi.

Peto.

Ego soror Katherina Knyghtly facio professionem, et promitto obedientiam deo omnipotenti, et beate marie semper Virgini, beato Augustino, et beate Birgitte, et tibi Confessori generali (vice illustrissimi domini collectoris) ex parte eorum, et tibi Abbatisse huius monasterii, et successoribus tuis, viuere sine proprio, et in obedientia, et castitate, secundum regulam sancti Augustini, et constituciones sancte Birgitte, reformatas, vsque ad mortem.

I Syster Katherine Knyghtly do make my profession and do promysse obedyence to almyghty god and to blessed mary always Virgin to blessed Saynt Austyn and blessed Saynt Birgitte and to thee generall Confessor (in steede of the popes Collectour) in their behalfe and to the Abbesse of thys monastery and to thy successors. to lyue without property and in obedyence and chastite accordyng to Saynt Austyns rule and the reformed constitucions of Saynt Birgitte vnto my deathe.

Assentior. 1612 . 2 Septembris

S Katharine Knightley

S. Anne wyseman. Abbes

Profession of Sr Katherine Knightley, 2 September 1612.
Exeter University Library MS 389/2937.

One further change that would have been felt acutely by the community every single day was the imposed discontinuation of the distinctive Bridgettine office. Henceforward, the nuns were to use the Roman Breviary, in the revised version completed and promulgated by Clement VIII in 1602.

———•——

Notwithstanding the constitutional uncertainties of these years, Syon was beginning to get itself established in Lisbon. Having spent its first five years in the city as guests of the Franciscans of Esperança, in 1599 the community was given the use of an adjoining property known as Sitio de Mocambo ('Mocambo Place'). It belonged to a Portuguese noblewoman, Izabella de Azevedo, widow of Luiz de Saa, who subsequently made the gift permanent, leaving them the site after her death in 1615. The abbey also benefited materially from the arrival of Leonor de Mendanha. The daughter and heiress of an important Portuguese noble family, she was in her twenties when she fled her mother and a projected marriage to join the Syon community in 1601, taking the name Sr Bridget. (She was one of very few Portuguese recruits to the monastery, which generally accepted only English postulants, a preference ratified soon afterwards by a charter of King Philip II.) Her family was initially hostile and resentful, but they were won over, and at her mother's death in 1616 the family estate passed to the community.

Building began, and the Convento das Inglesinhas (Convent of the Englishwomen), as it was known, began to take shape. Over the next twenty years, another fourteen choir nuns and six laysisters joined the community. Seth Foster recruited his nephew William Smith, who went on to succeed him as confessor general in 1628. His sister, Brigit, joined the nuns, as did their niece Mary Smith, who made her profession in 1643. As a dowry, Mary's father John Smith sent a shipload of wood, which was used in the building of the abbey church. The nuns later remembered it as 'a pretty composed, decent church'.[3]

Around the middle of the century the community weathered two major upheavals. The first was national. The dynastic union of the crowns of Spain and Portugal had lasted into its third generation, but during the reign of Philip IV of Spain (Filipe III of Portugal) tensions increased. On 1 December 1640 the Portuguese nobility staged a coup, stormed the Ribeira Palace in Lisbon, killed the secretary of state

Miguel de Vasconcelos, and acclaimed John, duke of Braganza, as King João IV of Portugal. The body of de Vasconcelos was thrown from a palace window into the street, where it was encountered by Syon's confessor general, William Smith (who seems to have inherited his uncle Seth Foster's knack for finding himself in the midst of political events): 'the Confessor, being down in the town, see[ing] the governor lie in the street without any human company, thought to [have] laid his mantle over him, but a gentleman of his acquaintance immediately went up to him and said it was not safe for him to take any notice'. Smith was subsequently arrested and interrogated, but once the authorities were satisfied that he did not pose a threat he was soon released. Nonetheless, the community, being now cut off from the patronage of the Spanish crown, was anxious for its future. Smith went to the new king to ask his leave to journey into Spain to seek the restoration of the community's pension. João IV asked the amount of the pension, before retorting that 'he was a king as well as King Philip': he would pay the pension himself, and the convent would remain in Lisbon.[4]

The second crisis was a domestic affair. On 18 August 1651 a laysister in the convent bakehouse apparently put some 'ashes into a basket not thinking that there was any fire amongst them'. But she was mistaken, and before long the nuns were roused by the cries of the townspeople. 'The poor religious being much fretted and surprised as may be imagined run about bare foot'; attempts to rescue anything from the flames were beaten back by the force of the fire. The convent was gutted, and most of the contents destroyed. The nuns were forced to seek temporary accommodation elsewhere. They received several invitations, but decided to take refuge, as they had on their first arrival in Lisbon, with their neighbours, the Franciscan nuns at Esperança. 'What a doleful spectacle had the poor religious to look on as they passed the church and house quite burnt down in a very little time', they recalled; 'in one hour to two it was laid in ashes.'[5] The fire had at least not reached the brothers' lodgings, so that they were able to remain, and soon afterwards the nuns rented some houses adjoining the Esperança convent, and set up a small chapel there for the brothers to minister to them. The accommodation was cramped and unhealthy, and there were tensions between the two communities, centring especially on Bridget de Mendanha, who by now had become abbess: some at Syon felt that she spent more of her time with her countrywomen from Esperança than she did with them.

Whatever the truth of that charge, the convent could not have been rebuilt so quickly without Abbess Mendanha. As a member of the Portuguese nobility, and a confidante of the regent, Queen Luisa, she was particularly well placed to solicit aristocratic patronage, while the brothers went out begging for charitable contributions from ordinary Portuguese. The foundation stone was laid on 2 December 1651, and the work was sufficiently complete for the nuns to return less than five years later, on 4 October 1656. Abbess Mendanha did not live to see that day, but shortly before her death in July 1655 she did manage to secure the future of another project. She was the driving force behind a new convent, founded as a daughter house of Syon, in the district of Marvila in the east of Lisbon. The Monastery of Our Lady of the Conception at Marvila (Mosteiro de Nossa Senhora da Conceição de Marvila) was a house for sixty Bridgettine nuns. As a counterpart to Syon's insistence on its English identity, and no doubt partly in response to Abbess Mendanha's own experiences, it would take only Portuguese women. The foundation charter was sealed in June 1655, and with a substantial endowment from the archdeacon of Lisbon, Fernão Cabral, the monastery opened in 1660, and continued successfully until its suppression in 1872. The chapel is now the parish church of St Augustine, Marvila.

Syon itself now entered on a period of stability. The restoration of the monarchy in England following the Civil War and interregnum meant that lines of communication between the abbey and the English Catholic community could be reopened. Indeed, when a couple of years later, in 1662, the new King Charles II married Catherine of Braganza, daughter of João IV, links between England and Portugal were as close as they had been at any time since the Bridgettines arrived in Lisbon. The daughters of English Catholic families started to arrive as postulants once more, bringing with them dowries to contribute to monastery funds.

And then, in 1697, gold was found in large quantities in the colony of Brazil, and the discovery ushered in a new age of Portuguese prosperity, and lavish development of the capital. Syon was already in the midst of some ambitious building projects of its own. First came the infirmary, built in 1683. Supervision of the work was entrusted to Sr Ursula Sutton, 'who was very dextrous in the forwarding of buildings for the community's comfort, and by what I have heard from all that knew her, above the common reach of women in those matters'. She was subsequently elected abbess and served three terms. During her abbacy a cistern was built in the centre of the cloister to supply the community with fresh water. It was completed in 1696 and may still be seen in the quadrangle, surrounded by the blue-and-white tiled arcading of the cloister. She was also responsible for the porches and grate house, and the verandahs. The latter caused some controversy. The project was expensive, and to fund the work Abbess Sutton sold off the books from the brethren's library (the last of the brothers having died a few years previously, as we shall see). There was also nervousness among the nuns over some demolition that needed to take place before construction could start, though Abbess Sutton had an answer for that. 'On one day when the community was all in the refectory at dinner, she set all her workmen to work in taking down those places which were in the way to make the verandahs square and handsome, and when the sisters came from dinner they wondered much at what she had done and in so little time'. Clearly another in the long line of strong women to have had the governance of Syon. The Lisbon annalist continues, 'I have often heard say and by several that knew her, that she was always after the workmen both late and early; neither could a piece of timber or stone be out of its place but she would immediately gather it up and put it by till it was wanted'.[6]

Work was done on the church, too, around this time. In 1707 a report described it as an impressive church of large size, with two side chapels on each side of the nave. The vaulted ceiling was lined with tiles and the walls were painted with brutesques – exuberant representations of animal and plant life that are a feature of the Portuguese baroque – as well as a Transit of the Virgin. Four large oil paintings depicting scenes from St Bridget's revelations had recently arrived, paid for by a bequest to Sr Mary Yard. The furnishings included a carved and gilded altarpiece and, in the upper choir, an image of the Virgin and Child that was reputed to have miraculous powers.[7] The church and some of the convent buildings, including the cloister with its cistern, may still be seen, in an imaginitive renovation by the architect Gonçalo Byrne opened in 2005, at the University of Lisbon's School of Economics and Management (ISEG).

———·———

If the convent buildings were taking solid and impressive shape, the make-up of the community they housed was changing. In 1607 Syon's revised constitutions were signed by Abbess Elizabeth Preston and nineteen sisters, and five brothers headed by the confessor general Seth Foster. The number of nuns, though never reaching the totals seen before the dissolution and exile, remained fairly constant at around twenty throughout the community's two centuries in Lisbon, maintained by a steady supply of postulants from England. It proved harder, however, to recruit brethren. In the new-look spiritual landscape of the seventeenth century, Catholic Englishmen could follow a scholarly vocation at the English University at Douai or enter one of the monasteries in exile, join the new order of Jesuits, or train as secular priests, to pursue an active role in the English mission. In such a context the distinctive charism of the Bridgettine brotherhood was not, perhaps, of obvious appeal or contemporary relevance.

We have already seen that Seth Foster persuaded his nephew William Smith to join him at Syon, before going on to succeed him as confessor general in 1628. Another recruit from this period was less of a success. Thomas Robinson was – at least by his own account, published in 1622 – a young seaman who, finding himself in Lisbon, made the acquaintance of Foster. The latter, by various 'subtle and wily fetches', persuaded him to remain, hoping (says Robinson) to have him as a brother of the house. What follows is a thoroughly scurrilous account of life in the monastery, in which Foster is the arch-villain, regularly enjoying rich food, raucous entertainments and the sexual favours of the nuns, whose poverty is a sham and their chastity non-existent. 'If I should repeat all their unchaste practices', Robinson confides, 'I should make the Christian reader blush at them: or if I should tell of all the obscene bawdry which I have seen, I might recount as many irreligious pranks as would fill a great volume.' In subsequent editions the work was provided with a frontispiece illustration, accompanied by some explanatory verses. On one side a nun is shown kneeling at the grate making her confession to the 'friar confessor'. On the other, the brother is opening the grate to let the nun climb through, and the

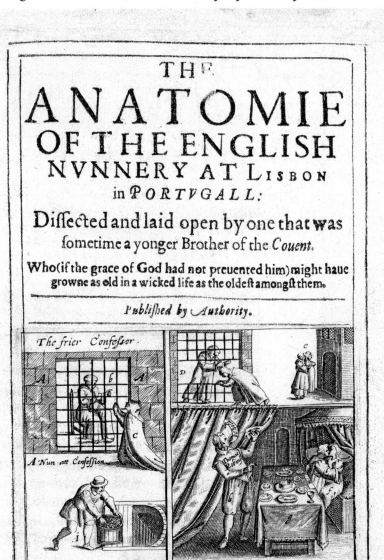

THE

ANATOMIE
OF THE ENGLISH
NVNNERY AT Lisbon
in *PORTVGALL*:

Diſſected and laid open by one that was
ſometime a yonger Brother of the *Couent.*

Who(if the grace of God had not preuented him)might haue
growne as old in a wicked life as the oldeſt amongſt them.

Publiſhed by Authority.

The frier Confeſſor .

A Nun att Confeſſion .

Printed for Philemon Stephens & Christopher Meredith. 1 6 3 0 .

Robinson's *Anatomie of the English Nunnery*
(London: George Purslowe, 1630), frontispiece.

two are walking together arm in arm. In the frame below, Robinson himself pulls a curtain aside to reveal a table laid with a banquet, and the brother and nun embracing on a bed.

> Thus have they reason England to deride,
> They do indeed fair chastity profess,
> Obedience, poverty, and seem no less:
> But God doth know, and Robinson can tell,
> All is beastly falsehood in this cell.

The pamphlet, entitled *The Anatomy of the English Nunnery at Lisbon*, sold well: a second edition was printed just a year later, in 1623, and it was issued again in 1630, 1637 and 1662. It belongs recognisably to a subgenre of anti-Catholic scaremongering that was popular in the seventeenth century, and especially in the early 1620s when a projected marriage between the future Charles I and the Spanish infanta seemed to presage an opening up of Anglo-Catholic relations. Robinson's prefatory address to the reader underlines the intention: 'if thou be not already addicted too much to Popery, thou mayst peradventure find a preservative against it'.

A copy of the pamphlet reached Syon soon after its publication, and in December 1622 someone from the community – most likely Foster himself – drafted a response. It is a raw and somewhat self-righteous document, characterised by a sense of wounded pride and embarrassed resentment at having been so easily taken in. It begins by discrediting the author – who, in this account, was a fugitive pirate who had imposed himself on the brethren under false pretences – before proceeding to a point-by-point refutation of the *Anatomy*'s catalogue of 'lies and slanders'. The effect of the response is not necessarily as its author intended: by taking every one of the *Anatomy*'s charges so seriously, he risked lending some credence to them, when a flat dismissal or disdainful silence might have been a better strategy. It was never published, which seems the right decision.

Libels like the *Anatomy*, of course, preached to the converted, stoking pre-existent anti-Catholic sentiment; it is unlikely that any potential Bridgettine brother's vocation was shaken by reading such slanderous material. The trouble was that the number of such vocations was dwindling. In 1672–3, when James Jenifer, captain of the Navy yacht

Suadadoes visited, there were twenty-eight sisters but the number of brothers had reduced to three. The captain found them to be 'three honest good fellows . . . whose happiness in living so pleasantly would almost prevail with one to turn Catholic'.[8] But unfortunately not enough of his compatriots concurred. There was never more than a handful of brothers, nor enough to perform divine office in the choir as Bridget had envisaged, and as had been practised in England. The community had to apply for leave to send brothers to England on a recruitment drive in 1634 and 1652. By the second half of the century, the situation was becoming critical. No brother of Syon was professed after 1663, when John Mark, a former Jesuit, joined the community, and he, in the event, did not stay: the Syon annalist reports that 'by some misunderstanding betwixt him and the abbess or some in the community he got leave of the nuncio and went from hence', returning to secular life.[9] When George Griffin was elected as the seventeenth confessor general in 1686, he was aged about sixty-five. There were two other priests, Jerome Blount and Robert Carlton, and two laybrothers, Laurence Mason and Peter Hall. The laybrothers both died in 1692, Carlton in 1693 and Blount in 1694. Griffin himself died on 24 June 1695, and with his death the Syon brethren came to an end.

The nuns, however, still needed the services of an English-speaking priest to say mass and administer the sacraments, and also, given the rebalancing of the roles of the abbess and confessor general in the 1607 constitutions, to take the lead in practical matters and relations with the outside world. Over the next twenty years or so the abbess engaged a succession of priests to provide spiritual services. One obvious source was the English College in Lisbon, but the College itself was struggling during this time, and its president grew exasperated at what he saw as 'poaching': 'These women are running mad for fathers', he exclaimed in 1714, 'and none will be fit for them but these that are brought up upon our cost and charges.'[10] Clearly it would be necessary to look elsewhere. The abbess wrote to the English Benedictine Congregation in Paris, and in 1717 they agreed to provide Syon with two monks, a chaplain-confessor and a procurator or administrator. Augustine Sulyard served as procurator until 1768, accompanied for the first eight years by Bernard Quyneo. Both men were warmly appreciated by the community; indeed, 'had two gentlemen been sought for there would not have been found two more proper to govern both spiritual and temporals than these two fathers was'.[11] Three other chaplains served successively alongside Sulyard until 1768, when the Benedictines, who were becoming over-stretched, pulled out of the arrangement. Now the English College stepped back into the breach, and the sacraments were administered by priests from the College, while its president seems to have acted, at least informally, as an adviser in temporal matters during the community's remaining time in Portugal.

———•———

Holding pride of place in the Museu Nacional do Azulejo (the National Tile Museum) in Lisbon is a panorama of the city viewed from the River Tagus. Composed of 1300 blue and white painted tiles, it is a little over 1 m high and almost 23 m long. It is a product of the early eighteenth century, the golden age of Portuguese *azulejos*, and a breathtaking work of art in its own right. But more than that, it is to baroque Lisbon what the Bayeux Tapestry is to Anglo-Saxon England: a monument, in the culture's most distinctive medium, to that culture's own passing. And, just as Anglo-Saxon England came to a violent end at Hastings, so the confident splendour of early eighteenth-century Lisbon ended abruptly in disaster. And the Syon community found itself in the middle of it.

Some time between 9.30 and ten o'clock on Saturday 1 November, the feast of All Saints, 1755, the nuns of Syon had finished their breakfast (tea and bread and butter) and Sr Catherine Witham (known as Kitty) was doing the washing up. Suddenly she heard a sound 'like the rattling of coaches' and 'the things before me danced up and down upon the table'. Her account, in a letter written to her mother almost two months later, is still full of breathless immediacy. She continues:

> I looked about me and see the walls a-shaking, and a-falling down, then I up and took to my heels, with 'Jesus' in my mouth, and to the choir I ran thinking to be safe there, but there was no entrance but all falling round us, and the lime and dust so thick there was no seeing. I met with some of the good nuns. They cried 'Oh run to the low garden'. I ask where the rest was. They said 'There', so (blessed be his holy name) we all met together, and run no further; neither had we any thoughts of running away further. We was all as glad to see one another alive and well as can be expressed.

Ruins of Lisbon as appeared immediately after the Earthquake and Fire of the 1st November 1755. Etching and engraving, after 1757. © Trustees of the British Museum.

Sr Catherine and her sisters were caught up in the Lisbon earthquake, an event whose scale, and effect on the contemporary European imagination, have earnt it the title of 'the first modern disaster'. The quake is thought to have measured in the region of 9.0 on the Richter Scale, about the same as the Tōhoku earthquake that took place off the east coast of Japan in 2011. Many of Lisbon's buildings collapsed immediately, killing some occupants, and trapping others in the rubble. Debris blocked the narrow streets, preventing survivors from escaping. Those who could get through ran to the city's public squares, and above all to the waterfront, where the boats moored on the river and the open spaces of the quayside seemed to offer a place of safety from the falling masonry. But, around thirty minutes after the initial quake, the first of three huge waves at least ten metres high came up the Tagus and smashed into the city, destroying the quay and sweeping away many of the people gathered there. Indeed the tsunami caused devastation along the Portuguese and north African coasts, and abnormally high waves were recorded from Cornwall to the Caribbean. And then there were the fires. They started with domestic fires and candles in destroyed or abandoned houses and, fanned by a brisk north-easterly wind, quickly spread and merged, until much of the city was in flames. People trapped by rubble burned to death, and those huddled with their salvaged belongings in the squares fell victim to what became an inferno. The fire burned out of control for the best part of a week.

Syon, at the western edge of the city, escaped the fire and tsunami, but aftershocks continued for several days. The nuns slept in the garden, at first under a pear tree covered with a blanket, later in a makeshift shelter made of wood. The convent itself was in ruins. Sr Catherine wrote:

> Out of five and thirty cells we have not one that we can lie in, till they are repaired. The church door has never been open nor mass said in it since. 'Tis so full of rubbish as also the choir and refectory and the kitchen entirely down, so we must do as well as we can till it pleases almighty God to send us a forturn.[12]

As for the rest of the city, 'Them that has seen Lisbon before this dreadful calamity and to see it now would be greatly shocked: the city is nothing but a heap of stones.'[13]

Above. Convento das Inglesinhas, Lisbon, from the north.
From [Manoel] Graïnha, *Histoire du Collège de Campolide et de la Résidence des Jésuites à Lisbonne* (Lisbon: A Editora Limitada, 1914), after p. 180.

Below. The cloisters, Quelhas Building (formerly Convento das Inglesinhas), Lisbon School of Economics and Management (ISEG), Lisbon.
Photo courtesy of Elizabeth Perry.

Modern estimates put the death toll from the Lisbon earthquake in the region of 15,000. (More were killed up and down western Portugal, and there were especially heavy casualties in Morocco, too.) Reconstruction began swiftly, however, under the energetic supervision of the prime minister Sebastião Jose de Carvalho e Melo, better known by his later title, marquis of Pombal. Pombal was a leading figure in the Portuguese enlightenment, and took the opportunity to rebuild Lisbon on rationally ordered and earthquake-resistant principles. But his efforts were concentrated in the *baixa* or downtown area of the city, and he was no friend of the religious orders (he had the Jesuits expelled from Portugal in 1759): Syon would have to fend for itself. With no prospect of alms from the stricken citizens of Lisbon, the community looked homeward for assistance. In May 1756 a petition was prepared and printed for distribution in England:

> We the underwritten, and company, having on the first of November last suffered such irreparable losses and damages by the dreadful earthquake and fire which destroyed this house and other parts of the kingdom, that we have neither house nor sanctuary left us wherein to retire; nor even the necessaries of life; it being out of the power of our friends and benefactors here to relieve us, they having all undergone the same misfortune and disaster …

they see no alternative but to plead for assistance from England, that 'we may for the present subsist under our deplorable misfortunes, and in time retrieve so much of our losses as to be able to continue always to pray for the prosperity and conservation of all our benefactors'.[14]

The petition had its desired effect, and the rebuilding of the convent was able to proceed quite quickly, in a plain architectural style without baroque embellishment. Not much more than five years after the earthquake they were visited by Joseph Baretti, the Italian-born English travel writer and member of the circle of Boswell and Johnson. There were twenty or so nuns who, he reports, welcomed all English-speaking visitors (whether Catholic or Protestant), and plied them with 'chocolate, cakes, and sweet-meats'. (Indeed, Baretti seems to have been impressed – because he repeats the reference – by 'that chocolate so plentifully distributed at their parlatory to their incessant visitors'.) This was a community apparently at ease with itself and in its surroundings:

Nuns in all countries are soft and obliging speakers, but these are certainly the softest and most obliging that ever fell in my way. Never was I told in a year so many pretty and tender words as this morning in half an hour.... In short, not a syllable issued out at their lips but what was dictated by modesty and meekness, humility and benevolence; and I will positively see tham as often as I can while I can stay here.[15]

Notes

1. *Wanderings*, ch. 54, 55.

2. Since 1580 Portugal had not had a nuncio (or papal ambassador) of its own. Instead, the papacy was represented by the apostolic collector, who ranked below the nuncio to the Spanish court in Madrid. After 1640 (when Portugal asserted its independence from Spain) there was again a nuncio to Portugal, and he assumed responsibility for the convent.

3. 'Lisbon Annals', p. 14.

4. *Ibid.*, p. 33.

5. *Ibid.*, pp. 34–7.

6. See *ibid.*, pp. 95–101.

7. http://www.monumentos.pt, and John Rory Fletcher, *The Story of the English Bridgettines of Syon Abbey* (South Brent: Syon Abbey, 1933), p. 127.

8. *The Manuscripts of the Earl of Dartmouth, Volume III*, Historical Manuscripts Commission, 15th Report, Appendix I (London: HMSO, 1896), p. 24.

9. 'Lisbon Annals', p. 85.

10. Simon Johnson, *The English College at Lisbon. Volume 1: From Reformation to Toleration* (Bath: Downside Abbey Press, 2014), pp. 342–3.

11. 'Lisbon Annals', p. 152.

12. *A forturn*: a turn for the better, an improvement in fortunes.

13. *English Convents in Exile, 1600–1800. Volume 3: Life Writing I*, ed. Nicky Hallett (London: Pickering & Chatto, 2012), pp. 309–10.

14. Aungier, *History and Antiquities*, p. *101.

15. *A Journey from London to Genoa* (London: T. Davies, 1770), pp. 193–5.

6

✛ *Return* ✛

Back in the second decade of the seventeenth century, King James I of England had begun to explore the possibility of a marriage alliance with Spain. By the early 1620s, a concrete proposal had been made for a union between his son and heir Charles and the Spanish infanta, Maria Anna, daughter of Philip III. Might a rapprochement with Catholic Spain lead to increased toleration for English Catholics? And could this be an opportunity for the exiles of Syon to return home? The community moved quickly to cultivate the friendship and support of the infanta Maria. They prepared a sumptuous gift for her: a manuscript account of their history, beautifully illustrated with scenes from their exile and peregrinations – scenes in which her grandfather Philip II features prominently as patron and protector. The volume opens with a petition to Maria signed by Abbess Barbara Wiseman and the convent of Syon:

> Grant us permission, Most Clement Princess, to hear us say (as also the people of Israel could say throughout the seventy years of their exile) that we know, feel and have experienced for more than seventy years the full hardships of this our exile; of which our many afflictions, sorrows, and tears are true witnesses and, without injuries, sufferings and dangers on land and at sea, true testimony of how much we have had to suffer; finally, the aching loss of our native land, families and mother tongue, as well as our extreme poverty in foreign lands and kingdoms, declare and make evident the burdens and great difficulties we have experienced and have carried on our shoulders.

Now, at last, the projected royal marriage seems to signal the divine intention 'to set us free, to put an end to our exile and lead us back to happy and greatly desired rest in our former home, Syon'.[1]

But the negotiations foundered, and the marriage never took place. Syon's exile would continue for a further two centuries. Through all this time, the convent maintained its sense of itself as a community in exile. It did this through the comparisons we have already seen to the Israelites in the wilderness; by the refusal (at least after the first decades) to accept anything other than English recruits, and to resist any other temptation to 'go native' despite the long sojourn in Portugal; by the maintenance of rituals and traditions, such as recitation of the *Martiloge*, that reach back to and recall the medieval Syon, and by physical mementos of the original abbey: books, the keys to the convent door, the Richard Reynolds pillar. At length, in the nineteenth century, the community's dream of a return to England was realised – albeit, as readers of the preceding chapters will not be surprised to learn, not without further trial and tribulation.

———

The Bridgettines would not be the first order to return to England. The majority of English monasteries in exile, we recall, had established themselves in northern France and the Low Countries. Although an early act in the French Revolution was the abolition of monastic vows and the suppression of contemplative orders (1790), English communities were, at this stage, exempt from persecution and dissolution. But in 1792 the English convents in France were closed down, and a few years later the occupation of the Austrian Netherlands by the revolutionary army also drove out the English-speaking foundations from those territories. During the 1790s more than twenty English communities returned from the mainland and attempted (with varying degrees of success) to re-establish themselves in Great Britain. Success stories include the Benedictine monks of Downside Abbey, exiled from Douai in 1794 and now based near Bath; the monks of Ampleforth, who can trace their lineage back to the Benedictines at Westminster Abbey under Queen Mary, and who have been settled near Wass in north Yorkshire since 1802; and their new neighbours, the nuns of Stanbrook, once of Cambrai, who relocated from their nineteenth-century home in Worcestershire in 2009.

Syon Abbey came close to being bracketed with those convents that failed to re-establish themselves, and died out within a few years of their return. Its eccentric location in Portugal kept the community from the immediate dangers and forced suppressions of the French Revolution, but not the political ambitions of Napoleon. His attentions first turned to Portugal in 1806. In November of that year he devised the so-called 'continental system', an attempted embargo on the import of British goods into mainland Europe. With most of the western European coastline in the hands of France or its allies, the blockade was almost complete. But the ancient alliance between England and Portugal – and in particular, the port of Lisbon – provided the British with a lifeline. With Spanish co-operation, the French army entered Portugal in November 1807, and captured Lisbon on 1 December. Queen Maria I, the prince regent, João, and the rest of the court had fled Lisbon a few days previously and taken ship for the colony of Brazil: Rio de Janeiro would replace Lisbon as the official capital of Portugal until 1822. Lisbon remained under French occupation during the first half of 1808, but in August of that year a British force under the command of Sir Arthur Wellesley (the future duke of Wellington) won a decisive battle at Vimeiro, to the north of Lisbon, and the French army was escorted from Portugal under British naval supervision. The British army, now under the command of Sir John Moore, advanced into Spain in an attempt to drive Napoleon's forces out of that country. But they were pushed back, and on 16 January 1809 at Corunna (A Coruña) on the north coast – despite a heroic rearguard, in which Moore himself was killed – they were forced to evacuate Spain altogether. The way was now open for a second attempt on Portugal, and in March the French mounted another invasion, taking the north-western city of Porto on 28 March, before preparing to march on the capital.

This is the context for the decision of Dorothy Halford, abbess of Syon, to leave Lisbon and return with the community to England. Abbess Halford received permission to leave from Cardinal Caleppi, the papal nuncio in Lisbon, but the community was not unanimous in its agreement, and those objecting had an ally in the president of the English College, James Buckley. Although the whole community went on board ship together, Buckley joined them there and – on the understanding that, now that they were no longer within the abbey enclosure, obedience to the abbess could be renounced – four nuns and three laysisters went with him back to the Lisbon convent.

On arrival in England, Abbess Halford and her remaining nine companions quickly made contact with a network of prominent Catholics. They were supported initially by Marlow Sidney of Cowpen Hall (Northumberland), a well-known friend of Catholic exiles. A few years previously, he had provided shelter to some Augustinian nuns from Cambrai at his London house, in Clarendon Square, St Pancras. The Suffolk antiquary John Gage of Lincoln's Inn (whose ancestors on his mother's side included the Gunpowder plotter Ambrose Rokewode) secured government pensions of £40 per annum for Abbess Halford and £30 each for the nine choir sisters. He also took the lead in raising money to help them get established in the capital. They had been staying in a small house at Walworth in Surrey, but in 1811 they were able to purchase a large brick house of three storeys in Peckham. They named it Syon House and started a boarding school for Roman Catholic girls. Two new choir sisters and two laysisters made their professions, though three of the nuns who had come from Lisbon died. By 1815, however, the project had foundered and they were forced to sell up. (In 1847 the former Syon House became Peckham police station, until it was demolished to make way for new premises in 1893.) Some of the nuns left, either for other religious houses or for secular life. Srs Monica Shimmel and Clare Butt decided to rejoin the community in Lisbon, though Butt died on the eve of their departure. (We are told that 'Some mischievous persons said she was poisoned; in consequence of which, after being buried three days, she was disinterred and examined to the satisfaction of all interested and concerned'.[2]) The five remaining sisters initially went back to Clarendon Square, and from there, in April 1822, to Cobridge Cottage, just north of Stoke-on-Trent (Staffordshire). Here Dorothy Halford (who had resigned as abbess soon after the return, in 1811) died on 16 June 1828.

By now, the group was in severe financial difficulty. They were rescued by John Talbot, the Catholic earl of Shrewsbury, of Alton Towers (Staffordshire). He found them new accommodation at Aston-by-Stone, also in Staffordshire, and provided each of the remaining sisters with a pension of £30 a year; in return, the nuns made over to him what was left of the ancient treasures they had brought with them from Lisbon. The arrangement suited both parties in the short term, but the last of the nuns died in 1837, and when Shrewsbury died in 1852, leaving no obvious heir, and his estate became the subject of a lawsuit of Dickensian proportions, the Syon legacy was broken up. Shrewsbury had already gifted some treasures away, and now others were sold and dispersed, including the keys to the monastery in Isleworth and the abbey seals, that had so defiantly been kept from Henry VIII's commissioners in 1539 (and whose whereabouts are now unknown). The best of the paintings went to Oscott College, the Catholic seminary at Sutton Coldfield near Birmingham. Some manuscripts came to the the dukes of Norfolk at Arundel Castle, including the beautifully illustrated account of Syon's exile described at the beginning of this chapter. Many were sold, including the fifteenth-century *Martiloge*, in which the community had continued to remember its dead well into the seventeenth century, which was bought by the British Museum and is now in the British Library. The famous Syon Cope, perhaps part of the vestments presented to the community by Archbishop Chichele on the occasion of the enclosure at Isleworth in 1431, ended up in the Victoria and Albert Museum. As recently as December 2013 an ivory sculpture of the Virgin and Child that had come from medieval Syon, and was listed in the Shrewsbury sale in the 1850s, reappeared and was sold at Sotheby's for a little over £2.5 million to a private collector. A few of these items later returned to Syon: the paintings were loaned back by Oscott College, for example, and the 1557 deed of restoration was presented to the community by George Charlton, grandson of one of the trustees of the Shrewsbury estates, in 1907. But most were lost for good.

History, of course, is written by the survivors, and it is easy to join Syon tradition in seeing Abbess Halford's as the false step. In such a view, her decision to leave Lisbon was the product of panic, and the return to England underprepared, and as a consequence it was destined to fail. Rose Macaulay, with a good deal of hindsight, calls Halford 'an impulsive and nervous woman', and tells us that 'those who stayed in Lisbon had rightly known that the precipitate flight would come to no good'.[3] But history, as ever, could have been otherwise, and in different circumstances we might, at this point in Syon's narrative, be celebrating Abbess Halford for her decisive action, whilst criticising the wilful disobedience of the nuns who stayed behind, and the unhelpful interventions of James Buckley in attempting to thwart her foresighted purpose. As it happened, the French army was forced out of Portugal in summer 1809, and when a final attempt on Lisbon in 1810–11 was repulsed by combined Portuguese and British forces under the duke of Wellington, Napoleon's armies had been driven out of Portugal for the last time.

Life in Lisbon, however, did not simply return to normal. The small group of nuns under the leadership of Sr M. Rose Lowe came back to find that their convent had been commandeered by the British army for a hospital. When they protested that they were few in number, poor, and one of them close to death, they were met with a gruff response: the commanding officer told them 'he cared more for one of his soliders than for all the nuns together'.[4] The group was taken in by the Irish Dominicans at Bom Sucesso in Belém. Sr Anthony Allen Gomes died there in January 1811 and is buried in the convent; it was several more years before the remainder of the community could return to their own monastery.

Even then, the future remained precarious. 'In 1816', the Syon annalist tells us, 'the community passed through severe trials. Sr Rose Lowe was very sick – vomiting blood and matter, and declared by the doctor to be living by miracle. Sr Constancia Sorrell was mentally afflicted, and Sr M. A. Kerby's mind had been weakened by her sufferings in a French prison, where she had been cast for religion's sake before she came to Lisbon; so that Sr Catherine Lake stood almost alone in the management of the house.'[5] But then five new postulants arrived from England, supplemented by another five the following year, and in 1818 they welcomed back their former colleague, Sr Monica Shimmel.

Portugal itself, however, took longer to recover. A country ravaged by war, ruled in name by a monarch resident nearly 8000 km away in Brazil, and in practice governed as a British protectorate, now began a process of long, convulsive and sometimes violent political and constitutional upheaval, that would, over the course of a century, transform it from an absolute monarchy into a republic. In the Liberal Revolution of 1820, progressive forces led by the Portuguese merchant class demanded the return of King João VI from Brazil, an end to British control over the government of the country, and the creation of a constitutional monarchy incorporating parliamentary democracy. The opposition between liberal and absolutist factions would set the tone for political strife in Portugal for a generation, and in the late 1820s, following the death of King João VI without a clear-cut heir, led to civil war. The liberals, with British and Spanish backing, took Lisbon in 1833, and the following year the civil war ended with the recognition of João's grand-daughter Maria II as queen and the establishment of a liberal constitution.

Portugal in 1834 may, at least temporarily, have been at peace with itself, but the war had left it bankrupt. The new government needed cash and wanted to bring about longer-term reform in land ownership; it was broadly anti-clerical in temper, and reserved particular enmity for the religious orders, which had tended to side with the conservatives during the civil war. And so it was that, three centuries after Henry VIII, Syon found itself living through another dissolution. On 28 March 1834 the new minister for justice, Joaquim António de Aguiar, declaring that 'The dominant opinion now is that religion does not benefit in any way from them and that their preservation is not compatible with the civilisation and enlightenment of the century', issued a decree suppressing all monasteries for male religious, and appropriating their lands and revenues to the state.[6] The monks were turned out without any effective provision for their support, earning Aguiar the nickname *Matafrades*, the Killer of Friars. Houses of religious women were spared the fate of the monks, but they were forbidden to profess new members, or to acquire or dispose of property, with the intention that, over time, they too would cease to exist.

The suppressions were preceded by rumours, threats and programmes of intimidation of a kind that the Syon community's sixteenth-century predecessors would have recognised. Government officials demanded access to the convent, taking inventories and examining accounts. On one occasion they were given two weeks' notice to quit the convent altogether, though in the event nothing came of the threat. Increasingly, the community was looking to Britain for protection and support. In July 1834 the nunneries in Lisbon were required to deliver up all title deeds and other materials from their archive to government officials. The Dominicans at Bom Sucesso did as instructed, only to regret it almost immediately: they managed to get their documents back only after protracted negotiation and with the assistance of the British embassy. The abbess of Syon refused to comply, stating her readiness to show any of the community's documents to the British authorities, but that she 'cannot deliver them up for inspection into the hands of the Portuguese, as she has good grounds to fear that they might be adulterated, retained or suppressed'. She appealed for the protection of the British ambassador, Charles Ellis, Lord Howard de Walden, writing to him with an expression of spirited defiance: 'The onus of showing that the monastery and property are not legal and English falls on those who are disposed to call this in question. When British subjects have been in pacific possession of property in this country for nearly three centuries, it belongs, not to them to show that this property *is* theirs, and consequently *British*, but to others to show that it *is not*.'[7]

Syon was allowed to continue, but the situation in Portugal remained volatile. A new bout of anti-religious sentiment erupted in Lisbon in 1857, with the arrival from France of a group of five sisters belonging to the Daughters of Charity of St Vincent de Paul, who intended to start a school. They were met with fierce and sustained opposition, to the extent that they had to be rescued by the French government, which in 1861 sent a warship to Lisbon to collect them. In April of that same year, a law was passed suppressing the last of the Portuguese convents for religious women. Syon, having established its identity as a British house, was exempt, but by now the conclusion was unavoidable: it was time to leave.

———————

Circumstances for a return to England were now considerably more propitious than they had been in 1809. The Roman Catholic Relief Act of 1829 had removed most of the disabilities imposed on Catholics over the preceding 250 years: they were now entitled to vote, and to hold most public offices. The number of British Catholics had been swelled by an influx of immigrants from Ireland, and there were some high-profile conversions from Anglicanism, including most notably John Henry (later Cardinal) Newman. In 1850, Pope Pius IX published a bull restoring the Catholic hierarchy in England and Wales. A diocesan structure was re-established, and twelve new bishops appointed under the archbishop of Westminster, Cardinal Nicholas Wiseman. The twenty or so religious communities that had returned to England around 1800 had been joined by an ever-growing number of new foundations. By 1880 there were more than three hundred convents in England and Wales. That number had increased to over 450 at the turn of the century, and by 1937 there were almost 1000 convents, belonging to 175 different orders and congregations.[8] In one important respect, however, the new foundations for women religious broke with medieval tradition. Where medieval nunneries had emphasised strict enclosure and withdrawal into a hidden world of silent prayer, the new orders and congregations of the nineteenth century were overwhelmingly active in their mission, the nuns and sisters engaged in outward-facing occupations such as nursing, social work or education. Already in 1857, two-thirds of the women's congregations and orders in England followed active vocations; by 1877 that proportion had risen to 80 per cent, and by 1937 it was virtually 90 per cent.[9]

Growth in the active congregations was especially strong in the areas of greatest urbanisation, and perhaps for that reason the predominantly rural south-west of England had a higher proportion of contemplatives than elsewhere. But it also reflected the personal efforts of the local bishop. The three south-western counties of Dorset, Devon and Cornwall made up the new diocese of Plymouth. The first bishop of the diocese was George Errington, but he left five years later to take up an appointment as co-adjutor to Cardinal Wiseman. His succssor, William Vaughan, would remain as bishop from 1855 until his death in 1902. Vaughan was from a prominent Catholic family; his nephew was Herbert Vaughan, later cardinal archbishop of Westminster. He oversaw the building of the cathedral, and is credited with establishing diocesan structures and administration in Plymouth. He also built up monastic life in the diocese, virtually from nothing. There were no convents in Devon when he took office in 1855.

At the moment when Syon was looking to leave Lisbon, Vaughan was already in advanced negotiations to bring another community to the diocese. The Benedictine nuns of St Scholastica's had been founded at Dunkirk in 1662, but returned to England following the French Revolution, and set up a school in Hammersmith. Now, however, the number of pupils had declined and they were looking to move away from London, and to pursue a more contemplative lifestyle. A site was found at Teignmouth, on the south Devon coast, and Bishop Vaughan laid the foundation stone for a handsome new monastery in the Gothic Revival style on 8 July 1862. Already resident in the diocese were the Augustinian canonesses of St Monica's Priory at Spetisbury in Dorset. They were another continental foundation, having been first established in the early seventeenth century at Louvain. They had been at Spetisbury since 1800, running a small school for Catholic girls, but since 1855, and with the strong encouragement of the newly appointed Vaughan, they had nourished a special attachment to the Blessed Sacrament, with a view to committing themselves to the practice of perpetual adoration. This devotion, which had grown popular among continental convents, especially in France, during the first part of the nineteenth century, involved the nuns in a round-the-clock vigil before the sacrament, which was permanently exposed. Through Vaughan's intercession, papal permission was granted and perpetual adoration commenced on the feast of Corpus Christi, 1860. (The nuns of St Scholastica's, Teignmouth, again with the active support of Bishop Vaughan, would follow suit and commit themselves to perpetual adoration from 1875.) This reorientation of the community from an active to a contemplative way of life was felt to necessitate a move to different, more secluded, premises, and the community quickly decided on Abbotsleigh House, on the outskirts of the village of Abbotskerswell, near Newton Abbot in south Devon. The property was bought in 1860 and, while building works were undertaken there, the canonesses began the search for a purchaser for the Spetisbury convent.

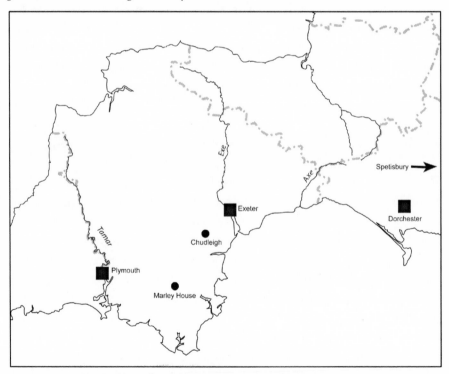

Syon in south-west England. © Oliver Creighton.

It was through Peter Baines, president of the English College at Lisbon, who had been advising them in temporal affairs, that the Syon community learned of the availability of Spetisbury. Bishop Vaughan was keen to have them in the diocese, and Baines (unlike his predecessor, James Buckley, in 1809) was fully supportive. The nuns began to pack. A lot had to be left behind, but they did carry with them two relics of the monastery in Isleworth that had accompanied them through all their wanderings: a large statue of St Bridget, and the fragment of pillar on which part of Richard Reynolds's body had been displayed in 1535. The date of departure was set for 27 August 1861. Bishop Vaughan sent Joseph Parke, a canon of Plymouth who had trained at the English College in Lisbon, to escort the party from Portugal to Spetisbury, where he was to become their chaplain. Some years later, Sr M. Bernard Eccles recalled the journey. After an early mass the nuns, dressed in mantles, hoods and face veils, were ready to leave. When the convent doors opened, 'crowds surrounded the convent, who had been waiting since three in the morning, and we could scarce get away, for the affectionate embraces of the multitude'. But 'the carriages were at last reached – and we were off!' They boarded the steamer *Sultan*, which took on another thirty or so passengers plus a mixed cargo of jewellery, wine, fruit and vegetables, and eighteen bullocks. After a short delay caused by fog in the English Channel, they landed at Southampton around noon on 31 August and, following prayers of thanksgiving for a safe journey and a meal, proceeded the forty miles to Spetisbury, where they arrived at around 3.30 in the afternoon.

The group that came to Spetisbury in 1861 consisted of the abbess, Sr M. Joseph Carter, seven other choir nuns, two novices and two laysisters. The price agreed for the convent was £3000 but the Syon nuns 'not being in good circumstances', the Augustinian sisters accepted £2200, on condition that the balance of £800 should be paid in the event of a subsequent sale.[10] Their new buildings at Abbotsleigh were not yet ready, so the two communities co-habited for a month or so, before the Bridgettines took sole possession on 2 October. They made a good impression on the canonesses, who recalled that 'we were greatly edified with their fervour and exactitude to their duties notwithstanding the smallness of their community'.[11]

Money was a problem. The community had left Lisbon without waiting for the convent to be sold. It would be several years more before it was bought by the Sisters of St Dorothy, a relatively new, active order, who used the buildings to run a school. Even then, it was difficult to get money out of Portugal. The sisters joked that at least, in their present circumstances, 'there could be no doubt about the practice of Holy Poverty'.[12] Though it ran against the spirit of their rule, they brought in a little income, as their predecessors the Augustinians had, by running a small school for the Catholic children of the village. Many of the necessities came by gift from benefactors: £15 from Joseph Weld of Lulworth Castle for a cow, and from other well-wishers crockery, refectory tables, and a kitchen dresser with pots and pans.

The premises at Spetisbury were never entirely satisfactory. The house 'was simply a very old secular habitation, much too large for us, and in an unhealthy situation, lying very low and subject to frequent inundations, caused by the overflowing of the river Stour, which passed along the bottom of the garden, thus rendering the house very damp'.[13] Early in 1883 the community was offered a newly built convent in

Convent at Spetisbury, late 19th century.
Reproduced from an old postcard, courtsey of Sue Stead.

Dumfriesshire, but the donor's insistence that the occupants should practise perpetual adoration of the Blessed Sacrament proved the sticking point: the Syon nuns were too old and infirm to make such a commitment, they decided. In 1885, however, they heard from Bishop Vaughan. Mary, wife of a prominent Devon Catholic, Evan Baillie of Filleigh, near Chudleigh, had expressed an interest in establishing a community of nuns there. Vaughan had recommnded the Bridgettines, and offered to take the Spetisbury premises in exchange for building them a new convent on the Baillies' land. On 14 December the abbess and Sr M. Catherine Green left Spetisbury, spent the night with their friends the Augustinian canonesses at Abbotsleigh, and on the afternoon of the 15th met the bishop at Chudleigh in order to choose the exact site for the new convent. They identified a spot just outside the village on Heathfieldlake Hill. First the ground had to be levelled and on 27 January 1886 the first turf was cut. In the spring Bishop Vaughan signed the contract for building the monastery, and nearly 300 trees were planted to form a boundary around the estate. The convent would contain twenty-seven cells, with a standard measurement of 9' × 8'7" (2.7 × 2.6 m), arranged over the upper two floors. The chapter house and library would be on the second floor. On the ground floor the cloister would surround a central quadrangle, and ranged around this would be the refectory, community room, laysisters' common room, and parlour. Domestic offices would be in the basement. The church was designed with the nuns' choir at right angles to the nave, so that the sisters and members of the public could both see the altar, without seeing each other. Near to the church, and just outside the front door of the convent, there would be a separate presbytery for the chaplain. By August things were taking shape: the large statue of the Blessed Virgin from the original Syon was sent to Chudleigh to be placed in a niche outside the building. Early in 1887, the cells were being furnished with an iron bedstead, a wooden chair, table, and a small washstand with cupboard beneath; the sisters were to be allowed to take with them the little chests of drawers that they currently had in their cells.

Abbess Carter did not live to see her community established in its new home; she died in April 1887, and Magdalen Heys was elected in her place. The next month, Bishop Vaughan wrote to say that work on the new convent was sufficiently advanced for the sisters to move in.

On 7 June the first load of luggage was sent ahead, and on the 16th an advance party of sisters led by the prioress set off for Chudleigh, where they were met by the bishop and Mrs Baillie: 'The latter had prepared a sumptuous repast for them and insisted on serving and waiting on the sisters herself'.[14] A little after 1 pm on 23 June the remainder of the community boarded the train at Spetisbury. They were met at Exeter by Canon Brownlow of Torquay, who took them for a cup of tea, before they continued by road to Chudleigh, arriving at 7 in the evening, to mixed feelings of excitement and dismay:

> Before retiring to bed we fully inspected every nook and corner inside the abbey. Outside it was impossible to walk, for bricks, mortar, and other rubbish, no walks, no shade of any kind, no trees worthy of the name. The refectory was our chapel for some time after our arrival, and the dispensary served as refectory.[15]

The first mass in the new church was celebrated on 7 August, but the stalls in the choir were not in place until December; the grille and grate for the confessional had arrived only in November.

Convent at Chudleigh, after 1925 (when it was purchased by the Redemptoristines).
Reproduced from an old postcard, courtsey of Chudleigh History Group.

But by the end of the 1880s the community had settled into life at Chudleigh. Additional land was acquired for pasture. (On 27 May 1892, the annalist tells us, the Jersey cow calved and the calf was named 'Beatrice of Syon.') On 4 May 1889 the community celebrated for the first time the feast of the Syon martyr, the newly beatified Richard Reynolds. Several new enterprises were begun. In 1893, with papal authority, Syon launched its 'Rosary Crusade', an 'association for the relief of the holy souls in purgatory'. The crusade was the brainchild of Sr M. Cecilia Keane, who had long been 'haunted by the thought of those countless souls who, in England alone, had been robbed, through the so-called Reformation, of the Holy Masses for which they had piously left endowments. What could she do for them?'.[16] Indeed, the crusade answered the broader question: now that (as we have seen) the overwhelming majority of nuns and sisters pursued an active apostolate, what was a contemplative order to do in and for the modern world? While other communities of nuns like their predecessors at Chudleigh the Augustinians, or the Benedictines of St Scholastica's at Teignmouth, had turned further inward and embraced the fashionable devotion of perpetual adoration, Syon saw in the crusade a purpose that accorded perfectly with its foundation as a chantry for souls. Members paid an annual subscription of one shilling, and undertook to pray a full fifteen decades of the rosary each week for the souls in purgatory; in return, weekly masses would be said for members living and dead at the lady altar of the shrine of the Rosary Crusade at Syon Abbey. The crusade was an immediate success: within a year subscriptions had paid for a new rosary altar in marble and alabaster, which was unveiled in a well-atttended public ceremony in May 1894.[17] Endorsed initally by Leo XIII, the crusade was reaffirmed by the new pope, Pius X, in 1903.

The community was intially more hesitant about its other new venture, into publishing. The idea came 'one morning in 1892', with a vist from Maurice Roche, curate at the Dominican priory church in Torquay, an early supporter of the crusade. In conversation with Sr M. Cecilia and the abbess, Magdalen Heys, he proposed that the crusade should be supported and advertised through the publication of a monthly magazine. The nuns' initial reaction was definite. "'Quite impossible," said Lady Abbess decidedly, and her companion agreed. "We know nothing whatever of the work of editors and should never dream of undertaking anything so ambitious and so utterly beyond us.'"[18] But Roche persisted and the first issue of *The Poor Soul's Friend and St Joseph's Monitor* appeared in March 1893. In an 'Introduction' to both the periodical and the Rosary Crusade, the prominent Jesuit and Church historian John Morris commends prayers for the holy souls in Purgatory, and the nuns of Syon for founding the crusade. 'It is', he says, 'not easy to refuse a request made by the Nuns of Syon', who have 'survived through all these centuries, to come back at last to England, and to take their place amongst us, the only representatives of an ancient English Religious House'. There follows an essay on Purgatory; an imaginative exhortation to pray for unknown souls who 'having suffered long in Purgatory, need one more prayer to set them free'; further stories and anecdotes; a piece excerpted from St Teresa of Avilà on the feast of St Jospeh (19 March), recently declared the patron and protector of the universal Church; the first instalment of a serial entitled *Aunt Betsy's Legacy* (which would continue through the next eight issues to no. 9 for November); a hymn to the holy face; 'A Corner for the Young' containing several songs and prayers; and notes relevant

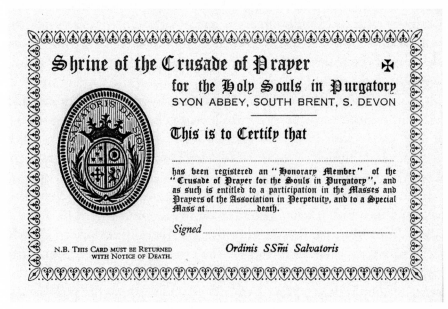

Membership certificate of the Rosary Crusade.
Exeter University Library MS 389, recently-acquired, uncatalogued box.

to the work of the associaton of the Rosary Crusade, including obituaries of associates or members. Subsequent issues would add testimony from members of the association of prayers answered, occasional book reviews, a competition to see which associate could recruit the most to the crusade, prayers, jokes and humorous snippets and, beginning in July 1893, 'Chapters from the Chronicles of Syon' by the Buckfast monk Adam Hamilton (who is introduced below). Later issues would include excerpts from the *Revelations* of St Bridget of Sweden, and from the abbey itself notes of professions, jubilees, sermons, and news from the monastery farm. The magazine had nearly two thousand subscribers by September 1893.

Securely re-established in England, the community now sought to re-establish some more aspects of its original identity. Soon after their arrival in Lisbon, we recall, the sisters had been obliged to give up the distinctive liturgy composed by St Bridget herself in favour of the newly standardised Roman breviary. Now, in January 1896, they petitioned Rome to be allowed to return to their traditional practice. In due course licence was received, and in May 1897 the nuns recited the Bridgettine office for the first time in almost three hundred years. Soon afterwards, moves were begun to restore the rule and constitutions of the abbey to something like their original purity, before the modifications that were introduced in Lisbon. At the same time, they could recognise the changes that had taken place in their community in the intervening period, not least the extinction of the Syon brethren. This process of revision and return resulted, in 1914, in a new translation of the Rule of St Augustine, St Bridget's Rule of Our Saviour, and the 'Syon Additions'. They were approved by Bishop Keily of Plymouth and published in a single volume in 1914.

In 1920, Syon celebrated the five hundredth anniversary of the first professions at the medieval abbey, and the beginning of community life. To mark the occasion the abbey published a little historical pamphlet by Dudley Baxter entitled *Five Centuries Record of the English Bridgettines of Syon Abbey, 1420–1920*. It gives a concise account of the community from its foundation until the arrival at Chudleigh, ending with the twin pious hopes that Syon should one day return to Isleworth, and Roman Catholicism to England, and asking, 'After such a record of half a thousand years, who can fail to recognize the manifest power of God, in Whose sight "a thousand years are but as yesterday, which is past, and as a watch in the night!"[19] A copy was sent to King George V and Queen Mary, who responded with a letter of hearty congratulations.[20] The quincentenary itself was celebrated on 27 July, with a visit from the archbishop of Westminster, Cardinal Francis Bourne. Two ancient privileges were restored by the Holy See. The community's devotion to a life of contemplation was given full recognition in the grant of papal enclosure and, by special licence from Rome, Sr M. Teresa Jocelyn and

Abbess M. Teresa Jocelyn.
From *The Poor Soul's Friend* 1945–6, frontispiece to Jan. 1946 issue (facing p. 177).

her successors were to be made perpetual abbesses, as their medieval predecessors had been. Abbess Jocelyn was installed in a ceremony presided over by the bishop of Plymouth John Keily on Wednesday 4 May 1921, by happy coincidence both the feast of St Richard Reynolds, and the eve of the five hundredth anniversary of the blessing of the first abbess, using 'the self-same ritual and prayers with which the first Abbess was blessed'.

During these years of consolidation and growth at Chudleigh the Syon community also made the acquaintance of three men who each, in his own way, played a key role in establishing the abbey's legacy. Adam Hamilton (1841–1908) was the only Englishman in the first generation of monks at the refounded Buckfast Abbey at Buckfastleigh in Devon, a dozen miles south-west of Chudleigh. Buckfast had been a Cistercian abbey in the Middle Ages, but the estate had been in private hands since the dissolution of the monasteries. A group of Benedictine monks who had been exiled from their own house in France acquired the site in

The community at Chudleigh in 1919.
Sr Anne Smyth, personal collection.

1882, and set about building a new monastery with their own hands, including a new abbey church on the original foundations. Hamilton was a frequent preacher at Syon, spiritual advisor to the nuns, and a keen researcher into their history. He contributed regular historical notes to *The Poor Soul's Friend* from its first year. His life of Richard Reynolds, *The Angel of Syon*, was published in 1905, and his edition of the *Wanderings of Syon*, our principal narrative source for the community's time in Rouen and the removal to Lisbon, was serialised, after his death, in *The Poor Soul's Friend*.

John Rory Fletcher (1861–1944) was a surgeon at Charing Cross hospital in London before his ordination to the priesthood in 1902. He first encountered Syon in 1922, on a visit to the then chaplain, who was an old friend. He quickly became a regular: 'a visit from Canon Fletcher was an annual event, generally in spring or early summer. He

Canon John Rory Fletcher.
Exeter University Library MS 389/1600.

loved the quiet of the country, the view from his windows, the wild flowers, the Devon air, and always seemed happy and at home'.[21] He devoted the years of his retirement to meticulous researches on the abbey's history, in the community's own archive and public records both in this country and abroad. His short *Story of the English Bridgettines of Syon Abbey*, published in 1933, and the excerpts from his more detailed history of the community that appeared some years after his death in *The Poor Soul's Friend*, represent only a fraction of his full achievement. This book (and especially chapter four) could not have been written without his manuscripts. Canon Fletcher died in 1944, after his London home was hit by a bomb, and by special licence he was buried in the cemetery at Syon.

The contribution made by the last of these friends of Syon was not a literary or historical one. Benedict Williamson (1868–1948) trained as an architect, and specialised in the design of churches, before his conversion to Catholicism and a somewhat ill-defined vocation to the religious life. He spent time as a Benedictine novice at Farnborough, and as a lay missionary to London's East End, before in 1904 he went to Rome to study for the priesthood. There he met Elizabeth Hasselblad, who was engaged in her plan to found a new, active branch of the Bridgettine order for women, and she suggested he attempt to revive the Bridgettine brothers. With a friend from his Farnborough days he began a community at Earlsfield in the London borough of Wandsworth in 1909 which made a promising beginning, but the project was interrupted by the War (Williamson served as an army chaplain between 1917 and 1919), and foundered thereafter. He was in touch with Syon from the outset (one of his novices in 1911 was Joseph William Ellis, whose sister was a nun at Chudleigh), and in the 1920s he served as their resident chaplain. In 1925, the community benefited from both aspects of his unique combination of skills when they moved to their new home at Marley House.

Notes

1. Christopher de Hamel, *Syon Abbey: The Library of the Bridgettine Nuns and their Peregrinations after the Reformation. An Essay by Christopher de Hamel, with the Manuscript at Arundel Castle* (London : Roxburghe Club, 1991), pp. 24–5. Illustrations from this manuscript appear on the cover of this book, and on p. 62.

2. 'Chudleigh Annals', p. 71.

3. *They Went to Portugal Too* (Manchester: Carcanet, 1990), p. 34.

4. 'Chudleigh Annals', p. 69.

5. *Ibid.*, p. 70.

6. Honor McCabe, *A Light Undimmed: The Convent of Our Lady of Bom Sucesso* (Dublin: Dominican Publications, 2007), p. 130.

7. Copy letter from abbess to lord Howard de Walden, 11 August 1834. Ushaw College Library, Durham, LC/A19/53.

8. Barbara Walsh, *Roman Catholic Nuns in England and Wales 1800–1937: A Social History* (Dublin: Irish Academic Press, 2002), p. 1.

9. *Ibid.*, Table 5 on p. 171.

10. 'Chudleigh Annals', p. 75.

11. Sue Stead, 'The History of St. Monica's Priory, Spetisbury, Dorset', https://sites.google.com/site/stmonicaspriory/.

12. 'Chudleigh Annals', p. 75.

13. *Ibid.*, p. 89

14. *Ibid.*, p. 95.

15. *Ibid.*, p. 97.

16. *Poor Soul's Friend* 1943–4, pp. 1–2.

17. *The Tablet*, 19 May 1894, p. 34.

18. *Poor Soul's Friend* 1943–4, p. 2.

19. *Five Centuries Record of the English Bridgettines of Syon Abbey 1420–1920* (South Brent: Syon Abbey, 1920), p. 24.

20. Exeter University Library MS 389/271, letter dated HM Yacht Victoria & Albert, 2 August 1920.

21. From his obituary, *Poor Soul's Friend* 1944–5, p. 29.

7

✢ The Final Century ✢

WITHIN A FEW YEARS of the celebration of their quincentenary, the nuns were looking to leave Chudleigh. In part, this was the result of success. Four novices had been clothed in 1923–4, and numbers were rapidly approaching Chudleigh's capacity of twenty-seven. In addition, the land on the opposite side of the valley had recently been sold for housing, and the convent and its gardens were now vulnerable to being overlooked, threatening the integrity of the nuns' enclosure. Then, in October 1924, Bishop Keily of Plymouth wrote to Mgr Arthur Hinsley at the papal curia as a matter of urgency: 'An ideal property has come into the market about ¼ mile away and can be got for a price that will not embarrass the Community. It is an ideal enclosure.'[1]

The property in question was Marley House, a large country house built in the eighteenth century in the parish of Rattery, near South Brent, a little less than twenty miles south-west of Chudleigh on the Plymouth road, and formerly a residence of the Palk Carew family of Haccombe in Devon. The estate was to be offered by auction at the Seymour Hotel, Totnes, on 20 March 1925. As members of an enclosed order, the nuns could not view the property before bidding. A small party comprising the prior of Buckfast Abbey and some of the monks, and Miss Dora Martyn, a long-standing friend and benefactor of the community, who was staying at Syon at the time, went to look around on their behalf, and brought back favourable reports. Application was made to Rome for the abbess to leave the enclosure to see it for herself, but on the morning of the sale, with the community on tenterhooks waiting for the crucial telegram, there was still no word. They made a last-minute decision to send Dora Martyn to bid on their behalf.[2] She returned having secured the house with eighty-seven acres for £5500. A few days later, the abbess received a letter of congratulation from Winfrid Recksteiner, one of the monks of Buckfast who had seen the

Above. The chapel at Marley House under construction.
From *The Poor Soul's Friend* 1926-7, facing p. 25.

Below. Aerial view of Syon Abbey, Marley House. Postcard, ?1970s.
Exeter University Library MS 389/2658.

property. The monks would be their new near neighbours. 'From all sides', wrote R. Dom Winfrid:

> I hear nothing but expression of satisfaction that the Syon Nuns are coming in our district and congratulating them on their splendid bargain. I feel confident that when you see the house and the property you will not repent of having taken the plunge without having seen with your own eyes and just acted on faith. I think the way it has come about is a sure indication that God wants you there, where you have an ideal spot for a contemplative order such as yours, quite by yourselves, and yet within easy reach, and where there is every prospect of development. Once you have a little Church of your own there, it will be a perfect little heaven on earth and a mirror of God's loveliness.[3]

Having thus obtained the site for a new convent, the community set about trying to sell their property at Chudleigh. Their preference was for a religious community to buy it, in part because of the duty to minister to the Catholics of the village that had been laid upon them as a condition of sale by Evan Baillie. The house with three acres of garden and twenty-five acres of pasture would be offered for £4500, the balance of the purchase price having come by gift from Dora Martyn. (Her special relationship with Syon was recognised by her acceptance as a sister of the chapter, and when she died in 1936 she was buried in the abbey cemetery.) Particulars were prepared and the abbess began writing to possible buyers. Her initial attempts drew a blank, however, and it was not until the Autumn that a purchaser was found. The Redemptoristine nuns of Clapham Park had found their solitude and seclusion threatened as greater London expanded outwards, and rural Devon provided an attractive alternative. They concluded the purchase and in November 1925 twenty-eight nuns moved in. (They remained at Chudleigh until 1989, when the premises were sold to a private buyer.)

In the mean time, work had been going on at Marley to prepare the house for its new occupants. A new wing was built adjoining the south-west corner of the main house, in typically plain Bridgettine style, to house the majority of the cells, and a presbytery was built on the other side. The architect was Syon's own resident chaplain, Benedict Williamson. The abbess and an advance party of four nuns left Chudleigh on 10 November, and the first mass in the temporary chapel at Marley House was celebrated by Williamson on Armistice Day, 11 November, 494 years to the day since the community had been enclosed at Isleworth in 1431. The remainder of the community arrived on the 22nd. 'Those days were indeed "great days"', recalled Williamson, 'crowded with incident, and of course, with not a little hardship and discomfort, but the nuns of Syon met this last move with the same joyous spirit with which they have met all those of the past. Indeed, these days helped one to realise better those early days of flight, when means of transport were scanty and enemies everywhere on the watch, and the way was indeed fraught with many dangers.'[4] Frost and rain hampered work on the conversion over the winter, and come the spring the chapter house and library were still doubling as a temporary chapel. The choir of the church proper was, however, starting to take shape; the guesthouse was under construction, and providing temporary accommodation for Williamson as resident chaplain. 'The nuns themselves', reported *The Poor Soul's Friend*, 'are nobly doing their part, staining and painting the woodwork, distempering the walls and whitening the ceilings of the existing building in the intervals between their solemn round of praise and adoration in choir.'[5] With financial support elicited through an appeal in the magazine, work continued throughout 1926. On 27 April Marjory Hutchinson of Exeter was the first to receive the Bridgettine habit at the new Syon Abbey. The church was blessed on 5 September, and a date of 28 October was fixed for the community's solemn re-enclosure. In the run-up to the ceremony the abbey received numbers of curious visitors, 'asking and receiving permission to be shown what they would not see again'. At 2.45 pm on the 28th, a bell sounded and the visitors joined the community and clergy in a procession that took them from the church, upstairs and through the cells, down to the chapterhouse and noviciate, and thence to the door of the enclosure, where visitors and clergy continued in procession back to the church, while the community remained behind and the abbess locked the door.[6]

And so the quiet, hidden round of Bridgettine observance resumed. A few years later, Canon Fletcher concluded his *Story of the English Bridgettines* with an idyllic portrait of the community peacefully ensconced at Marley:

Here in Devonshire as one looks down upon the abbey from the drive it appears to be the very emboidment of peace and security. Is then the wandering of Syon at an end at last? Who knows? It will be as God pleases. One can say, however, that the situation of the present convent is an ideal one for an enclosed Order, secluded, healthy, with an extensive enclosure, and around it glorious scenery. Here between the quiet Devon hills Syon keeps watch, observing all the details of the religious life as handed down from the days when the Bridgettines pursued the same rule of life within the great monastery at Isleworth; and in the round of religious observance at Marley to-day we can see the same ceremonies as the Syon community followed five hundred years ago.[7]

During 1914–18 the nuns had been licensed to leave the enclosure at Chudleigh to help cut hay, but the Great War had not otherwise significantly impinged on their quiet existence. World War II, by contrast, made its daily presence felt at Syon, as at many another big house in the English countryside. In 1939 two 'pillboxes' were built on Syon property as part of the defences against a possible German invasion. The nuns were instructed to plough up some of their pasture, and put the garden down to potatoes and roots, as part of the campaign to 'dig for victory'. In 1940, at the height of the Blitz, the house was being talked of as a possible refuge for children evacuated from London, though in the event no-one came. In the months prior to D-Day, the US army was installed in a camp that was set up in one of the fields. Some of the soldiers would come to mass in the abbey chapel, and impressed the nuns with their singing, not to mention 'the melodies from *Annie get your Gun*, played on the Camp's loudspeaker system (which could be heard inside the Abbey).[8] The camp was subsequently used for German and Italian prisoners of war. They too sometimes attended mass, and many years later the community still remembered their lusty singing as they joined in the hymns.[9]

Although the name 'Camp Field' stuck, in other respects Syon returned to normal after the War. But at the same time, the far-reaching social and technological changes that were its legacy would set the tone for the increasing secularisation and the general decline in numbers of the religious orders that characterised the second half of the twentieth century, and to which in time Syon itself would fall victim.

Marley House, with its grand, porticoed front, gives an undoubted impression of splendour, but most of the comforts and conveniences of modern life were wanting. Behind the facade were all the difficulties of living in and maintaining a large, historic building, while the nuns fought a running, and as the years went on increasingly futile, battle against a chronically leaking roof. Life was basic. When Abbess M. Teresa Jocelyn, who had overseen the move to Marley, died in 1946 an appeal was launched in *The Poor Soul's Friend* to raise money for a fitting memorial to her. After some deliberation the community decided to use the proceeds to replace the existing gas lamps with electric lighting, and to install central heating in the church. There is some dry Syon humour here: the formidably austere Abbess Jocelyn was known for her refusal to allow the closing of windows even in the frozen depths of winter. Perhaps she had the last laugh, though: the new heating system was completed in early summer 1949, in the midst of a heatwave. It had to be run continuously for four days for testing: 'Talk about Purgatory', recalled the nuns; 'I think we had a good taste.'[10] It was another twenty years or so before mains water arrived. Before that, water had come from a pair of small reservoirs on the estate, and had

Marley House, front, *c.* 1950.
Exeter University Library MS 389/3704.

to be carried upstairs in buckets. Frozen in winter, in some summers it would run dry altogether. The ancient (and originally second-hand) Aga finally made way for a modern gas stove in 1972. And it was only in the late 1970s, after the bishop's visitor had warned them that the true purposes of Syon's foundation were in danger of being submerged by the sheer quantity of domestic work, that the sisters purchased a dishwasher, vacuum cleaners and a floor polisher.

Advances in technology largely passed the community by during the first half of the twentieth century, though the abbey's isolated position made a telephone a necessity. In 1931 the editor of *The Poor Soul's Friend* told that magazine's readers, 'It is hardly necessary to say that wireless is not part of the equipment of Syon.'[11] Twenty years later, when the Dominican Esmond Klimeck, a fellow promoter of the rosary prayer, visited, he brought with him a statue of Our Lady and a film he had made of the site of the apparitions at Fatima in Portugal: 'It was an interesting experience as many of the Community had never seen a film.'[12] A few years later, however, a television was hired for the day so that the nuns could watch the coronation of Pope John XXIII in 1958, but the community did not have its own set until a few years later. By the late 1960s, the nuns were listening to talks on tape on scriptural and theological subjects in place of the traditional reading in refectory at supper time. In the 1990s, a computer was acquired for letter-writing, account-keeping and email, though Syon never emulated Vadstena by hosting its own website.[13]

At the beginning of 1959, only a few months after his election, Pope John XXIII announced his intention to call a general council of the Roman Catholic Church. The last such meeting (itself the first since the Council of Trent) had been held at the Vatican in 1869–70, but had been cut short when Rome fell to the forces of the newly unified Italian state. The challenges facing the Second Vatican Council were less political and theological – it did not, for instance, find itself having to condemn any heresies – but more the question of how far the Church should try to respond to the social changes of the post-War world. Pope John spoke of an *aggiornamento*, a bringing up to date, and opening the windows of the Church to let some fresh air in. The council opened on 11 October 1962. (The nuns of Syon again hired a television set for the day so that they could watch the opening ceremony.) Although John XXIII died the following year, the work of the council continued under his successor Paul VI and concluded in December 1965. Its constitutions and decrees brought about a wide-ranging (and in many cases still controversial) revolution in Catholic practice that included a new openness to dialogue with other religions and confessional traditions, a simplification of the liturgical calendar with the removal or downgrading of many traditional feasts and observances, increased participation of the laity in the work of the Church, and a radically new experience of the mass: the celebrant henceforward would face the congregation, vestments and church furniture and decoration would be simpler, the music modern, and the language used typically the vernacular rather than Latin.

The changes were felt at Syon. In October 1966 Sr M. Barbara Hunt made her first (simple) profession, and the traditional Bridgettine rite was translated into English for the occasion. 'This was the first time that our ancient Profession ceremony had been performed in English', the community reported, 'and great care had been taken beforehand to see that all present were provided with the English text and music. The whole ceremony, carried out with simplicity and dignity, brought its meaningfulness into a new light which was much appreciated by all who were present.'[14] At Christmas that same year, English was used for the first time at midnight mass, to a similarly positive reception: 'The spirit of Christmas joy and the spirit of renewal which the Second Vatican Council asks of us all in celebrating the Eucharistic Liturgy, reigned in abundance!'[15]

As well as encouraging the use of the vernacular languages in the liturgy of the mass, the decree 'Sacrosanctum concilium' (4 December 1963) also permitted religious communities to recite the divine office in an approved translation. At the same time, it abolished the night office, by suppressing prime, and allowing communities to recite matins at whatever convenient time of the day they chose. In response, the Syon breviary was simplified and revised: matins, with its readings in honour of the Virgin Mary that are the most distinctive feature of the Bridgettine office, was renamed the office of readings, and henceforth would take place in mid-afternoon. Meanwhile, the whole of the office was translated into English by Fr Brian Foley, Barbara Hunt's parish priest at Clayton Green, near Preston in Lancashire, and a notable musician and hymnodist. The translated office was complete by the end of the 1960s, and has been prayed by the Syon community ever since.

Vatican II also addressed directly the place of the consecrated religious life in the Church. The 'Decree on the sensitive renewal of religious life' known (from its opening words) as *Perfectae Caritatis* reasserted the role and value of the religious orders as 'a vital force in today's world', but also called for 'the sensitive renewal of the life and rule of religious bodies'. Renewal would involve 'the constant return to the sources of christian life in general, and the original genius of religious foundations in particular; together with the modifications of such foundations to accommodate new circumstances'. Declaring that 'the style of life, prayer and work of the modern religious should reflect contemporary ideas and living standards', the decree called for each order's constitutions, rules, and so on to be 'carefully scrutinised' in the spirit of the council. Recalling the common life of the early Church, the decree required nunneries to phase out the laysisterhood. Although papal enclosure was still to be permitted for contemplative orders, communities were encouraged to ask themselves whether strict enclosure remained appropriate to their 'charism' or distinctive calling and character. The habit was to be re-examined with an eye to 'the demands of hygiene, the style of contemporary fashion, and the practicalities of the apostolate'. Throughout the process, the emphasis was to be on 'abolishing dead customs', in an attempt to achieve the 'harmonising of religious life with the demands of contemporary society' whilst reasserting the essential principles of chastity, poverty and obedience, of which 'Christ himself, the lord, is the model'.[16]

The council reaffirmed the place of the wholly contemplative foundations but did not, however, exempt them from the spirit of renewal that it espoused. In a follow-up letter, *Ecclesiae Sanctae* of 6 August 1966, Pope Paul encouraged all religious institutes, including the contemplative orders, to 'first of all promote a spiritual renewal, then prudently and without delay proceed to the appropriate renewal of their life and discipline'. At Syon, the nuns decided that any modernisation of the habit should respect its most distinctively Bridgettine features: they dispensed with the mantle (the heavy monastic cape), but retained the crown with its symbolism of Christ's five wounds. Likewise, they

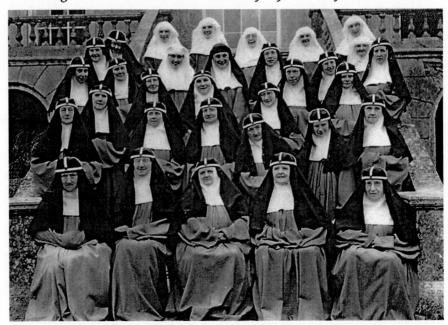

Above. The community in 1961. From *The Poor Soul's Friend* 1960-1, p. 178.

Below. The community in 1982.
Photo by Harold J. Deakin. Sr Anne Smyth, personal collection.

Above. Nuns knitting, 1982.
Photo by Harold J. Deakin. Sr Anne Smyth, personal collection.

Below. Sr M. Cecilia in the cemetery, 1982.
Photo by Harold J. Deakin. Sr Anne Smyth, personal collection.

determined to maintain papal enclosure, but the forbidding wooden grille was removed from the chapel, and those in the grate rooms were fitted with sash cords so they could be opened or closed at will. (When the new Syon Abbey was constructed in 1989–90, as detailed below, it was built without grilles at all.) Henceforth it would be sufficient for the nuns' separation from the world to be marked by a continous low partition.

The process of revising the constitutions began. In 1969 Dr Peter Rutten was delegated by Rome to work with Syon and the two Dutch Bridgettine houses, Uden and Weert. Vatican II had encouraged smaller, independent communities to consider entering into federation, and the three convents were expected to consider the possibility. In July 1970 Abbess M. Peter Wallace, accompanied by Sr Anna Maria Smyth, left the enclosure and travelled to Holland to discuss plans with Dr Rutten and representatives of the other houses, but in the end all sides agreed to maintain the Bridgettine tradition of autonomy. The first draft of Syon's revised constitutions was submitted to Rome in 1974. The document is true to the spirit of Vatican II in its attempt to get back to the essence of Bridget's rule, rather than getting mired in incidentals. Language of prohibition and discipline is replaced with positive evaluations of the essential vows of chastity, poverty and obedience; enclosure features not so much as a defence against the dangers and temptations of the world, but as an enabling precondition for the life of contemplation. The changes required to the draft constitutions were mostly minor and technical, but time-consuming; the resubmitted document was approved in February 1980, initially for a trial period of seven years, after which it received final confirmation.

———•———

A handful of nuns left Syon in the years immediately following Vatican II, and (as was the case in many religious orders and congregations) the changes brought in by the council were a factor in several of those cases. But declining numbers had already been an issue for some time. In September 1926, Winifred Kelly made the first solemn profession in the new abbey church at Marley House, becoming Sr M. Katherine. Another solemn profession followed in 1927, two in 1929, two more in 1931, one in each of the four years 1933–6, another in 1938, two in 1940, then 1945, 1946, 1948, 1949 and 1950, before a three-year gap until the next profession, in 1953.[17] The subject of vocations – both to the priest-hood and religious life in general, and to Syon in particular – starts to come up regularly in *The Poor Soul's Friend* in the period after the War. As early as 1949, the community was making its prayers for new recruits to St Jude, patron of hopeless cases, and the following year they noted 'Now we have plenty of choir Stalls empty for Postulants', adding a plaintive 'Are there none of our Readers who have daughters or friends willing to consecrate themselves to the life of Praise of the Holy Mother of God?'[18] The 1953 issue included a direct appeal from the abbess herself: 'Any young woman of normal good health who wishes to consecrate herself to God in the contemplative life, to sac-rifice herself for His glory and the praise of His Blessed Mother, will find what she desires in the peace and seclusion of Syon Abbey in the beautiful Devon country.'[19]

It is telling that, in the regular updates from Syon in *The Poor Soul's Friend*, as the twentieth century goes on, the silver and golden jubilees start to outnumber the professions. Later in the century, it is the obitu-aries. New nuns took their solemn vows to become full and irrevocable members of the community in 1954, 1955 and 1960, but when in 1962 Hilary Cotton became Sr M. Bridget, hers was the last solemn pro-fession to be made at Syon, though two nuns from other Bridgettine houses transferred to Syon after that date. A number of women were accepted as postulants, and two made their first or simple vows (one in the 1960s, the other in the 1980s), but they did not go on to make their solemn profession and become permanent members of the com-munity. Syon's experience was not unusual. Most British orders started to struggle for recruitment from the 1950s onwards. In 1950 there were 84 male religious and 1160 female in the diocese of Plymouth. By 2000, those numbers were 58 and 198; and in 2013, there were only 90 female religious left in the diocese, less than a tenth of the figure a half-century earlier.[20] The Augustinian canonesses at Abbotsleigh closed in 1983, and the Benedictines of St Scholastica's at Teignmouth in 1987.

In 1961, when the Syon community celebrated the one hundredth anniversary of its return to England, there were twenty-six choir sis-ters (including two novices) and six laysisters. By 1974 the community numbered eighteen, of whom only seven were under the age of seventy. The decision was taken to cease publication of *The Poor Soul's Friend*

Above. The new convent under construction, 1989.
Sr Anne Smyth, personal collection.

Below. Sr M. Gabriel inspects the work in progress.
Sr Anne Smyth, personal collection.

The completed new convent.
Sr Anne Smyth, personal collection.

(since 1968 known instead as *Syon: Magazine of the Crusade of Prayer for the Faithful Departed*), in part because of rising costs, but also due to falling human resources: though the crusade and magazine had seemed to accord well with the abbey's original function as a chantry for souls, the abbess wrote, 'times change and people change and now it seems that the Community could become bogged down by commitments we are not able to fulfil'.[21]

By the mid-1980s it had become clear that the present convent buildings were no longer a practical or suitable home for an aging and shrinking community. One possible solution was to divide the accommodation so that it could be shared with another group of contemplative nuns. Architects were consulted on the work that would need to be done, and Abbess Anna Maria Smyth wrote to each of the ninety-five enclosed communities then extant in Great Britain, but those who replied all wrote to say that they found themselves in similar or worse straits, and were in no position to consider a move. By February 1987 Fr Alan Robinson SJ, vicar for religious in the diocese of Plymouth and Syon's resident chaplain, was recommending to the nuns that 'we should seek a radical solution to our problem of a decreasing number of sisters living in a very large building.'[22] But they did not want to leave Marley. The solution came to Abbess Smyth during an afternoon walk that Easter Sunday: the old stables and shippen at the end of the farm track could be converted into a new, purpose-built convent. To see their potential required a degree of vision. The architects who eventually carried out the conversion recalled their first impressions: 'The farm buildings presented a forlorn picture, needing a good deal of repair even to allow them to continue in their current use.'[23] But a feasibility study and enquiries of the planning office were encouraging, and plans were drawn up. The existing buildings were arranged around a yard, and these could be extended to form a quadrangle. One range would house the communal rooms, while the other, over two storeys, would be divided into nine cells and a flat for the resident chaplain situated above the small chapel.

Marley House was offered for sale with fifty-five acres early in 1989. Tenders were received proposing conversion to a hotel, a training and conference centre, offices and company headquarters, a sports and country club, timeshare accommodation, an old people's home, a motorway service station, and a 'working village' development including housing and workshop units. In the end, an offer for just under £1m was accepted from a local man who intended to turn the house into a hotel and the grounds into an eighteen-hole golf course. Contracts were exchanged in July for completion in October. But the financial crisis that followed the UK's abrupt exit from the European Exchange Rate Mechanism that Autumn, and the consequent collapse of the housing market, saw the buyer unable to complete. The property was put back on the market, but it would be 1993 before a sale was finally concluded. Marley House was divided into seven apartments with communal gardens and grounds, the 1920s extensions were demolished and replaced by eight newly built houses, and two small cottages were converted, giving a total of seventeen dwellings on the site.

Back in 1989, however, the community found itself with its sale having fallen through, but committed to the move to the new convent. With the help of bridging loans, work began on 12 December 1989. The nuns took a close interest in the conversion, going down the farm track from the abbey in the evenings after the workmen had left to see how work was progressing. The architects recalled that 'the sisters made enthusiastic, interesting and tolerant clients'.[24] Much of the contents of Marley House had to be disposed of. Furniture (over one hundred lots) and works of art (more than one hundred and fifty) were sent to London for sale; most of the eighteenth-century paintings went back to Oscott College, while the collections of manuscripts and early printed books were deposited with the library of the University of Exeter. The first boxes were moved, appropriately enough, on the feast of St Bridget, 8 October 1990; a week later the nuns spent the first night in their new cells, and on Tuesday 16th mass was said in the chapel for the first time.

————•————

A few years later, in 1993, Sr Patricia of Vadstena Abbey contributed to a collection of scholarly essays on St Bridget and her order. She remarked,

> It is difficult to write about the present time. There is no perspective, just the blunt confrontation with the fact that today is not the day for young people to enter religious life. At least, not in Western Europe. The times are uncertain. All the old, firm standards have fallen and the new have not yet taken form when they too are whisked away. Religious life, as such, seems rather an anachronism along with other stable relationships. . . . This is a problem for the few remaining medieval communities in Saint Birgitta's Order. Each of the older houses is confronted with the problem, too few nuns, all of them elderly, and no candidates coming in. The future is in God's hands. Each of these houses have experienced this same problem many times during their long and varied histories. None of them intend to give up, not yet.[25]

But, with an inevitability that Sr Patricia clearly realised, by 2005 the Syon community was planning for a future that included the closure of the abbey. The youngest of the four remaining nuns was 67, and the oldest, Sr M. Veronica, had left the enclosure and was being cared for by the Sisters of Nazareth at Plymouth. The abbess entered into detailed discussions with the diocese, declaring that the community's reduced numbers left them unable to fulfil all the norms and requirements of their constitutions, whilst expressing 'our wish and sincere hope that we may be permitted to continue our contemplative religious life as a Bridgettine community for as long as we are able to do so, health and other factors permitting'.[26] A petition was submitted to the Congregation for Institutes of Consecrated Life in Rome, and in 2007 permission was granted that, when the time was deemed to be appropriate, the nuns might transfer to Nazareth House in Plymouth.

The winters were hardest. After the severe winter of 2009–10, December 2010 was the coldest since UK records began. The temperature in Devon fell to an all-time low of −16.5° C on 26 December, and on several occasions heavy snowfall closed the A38 Exeter–Plymouth trunk road. At Syon, an order for liquefied petroleum gas that had been placed at the beginning of the month failed to arrive, the adverse weather having disrupted supplies nationally,[27] and on Christmas Eve the central heating ran out. The community got through the winter but, as a result of the experience, and faced with the rapidly declining health of one of the three remaining nuns, they knew that the time had come. They announced their decision in early April, and the convent went on the market just before Easter.[28]

Although there were enquiries from several religious communities, in the end an offer was accepted from a woman who intended to use the premises as a dwelling, and to run it as a venue for multi-faith (and no-faith) retreats. The abbey's archive was transferred to Exeter University for safe-keeping; the church plate and relics went to Buckfast Abbey, while the stone pillar from the gatehouse of the medieval Syon Abbey on which part of St Richard Reynolds's body was said to have been displayed found a new home at the church of the Blessed Sacrament at Heavitree in Exeter, near the suburb of Pinhoe where Reynolds is thought to have been born. The nuns themselves left the convent soon after they had celebrated the mass of thanksgiving on 6 August, one into care, the remaining two on 7 September 2011 to Nazareth House in Plymouth, where they maintain their Bridgettine observance to the present day.

The Final Century

Notes

1. Exeter University Library MS 389/1066, copy letter of 15 October 1924.

2. Exeter University Library MS 389/159, copy letter Sr M. Aloysius to Bishop Keily, 25 March 1925.

3. Exeter University Library MS 389/1066, letter of 26 March 1925.

4. *Poor Soul's Friend* 1925–6, p. 291.

5. *Poor Soul's Friend* 1926–7, p. 4.

6. *Ibid.*, p. 229.

7. Fletcher, *Story of the English Bridgettines*, pp. 162–3.

8. *Syon Abbey* 1968–70, p. 140.

9. *Syon Abbey* 1972, p. 32.

10. *Poor Soul's Friend* 1948–9, p. 124.

11. *Poor Soul's Friend* 1931–2, p. 252.

12. *Poor Soul's Friend* 1951–2, pp. 163–4.

13. http://birgittaskloster.se.

14. *Poor Soul's Friend* 1967, p. 7.

15. *Ibid.*, pp. 38–9.

16. Quotations in this paragraph are taken from Norman J. Tanner, *Decrees of the Ecumenical Councils: From Nicaea I to Vatican II* (London: Sheed & Ward, 1990), pp. 939–47.

17. See the list of professions in Exeter University Library 95/18.

18. *Poor Soul's Friend* 1948–9, p. 183.

19. *Poor Soul's Friend* 1952–3, p. 121.

20. Figures from http://www.catholic-hierarchy.org.

21. Exeter University Library MS 389/612, copy letter Abbess Smyth to Bishop Restieaux, 16 April 1974.

22. Quoted by Abbess Anna Maria Smyth, uncatalogued letter to J. Cunningham, 17 November 1988.

23. David Mansfield Associates, report in *Church Building*, Autumn 1991, p. 24.

24. *Ibid.*, p. 25.

25. 'The Present Time', in *Studies in St Birgitta and the Brigittine Order*, ed. James Hogg (Salzburg: Institut für Anglistik und Amerikanistik Universität Salzburg, 1993), ii.102–6, p. 102.

26. Letter to Kristian Paver JCL, Presbytery, Totnes, 7 Nov 2005. Exeter University Library MS 389, recently acquired box, uncatalogued.

27. *You and Yours*, BBC Radio 4, 22 December 2010.

28. *The Tablet*, 9 April 2011.

Abbess Anna Maria Smyth and the Rt Rev. Christopher Budd,
bishop of Plymouth, at the Mass of Thanksgiving, 6 August 2011.
Sr Anne Smyth, personal collection.

SUGGESTIONS FOR FURTHER READING

I have tried not to weigh the text down with scholarly footnotes. Instead I list here the principal sources that I have drawn on for each chapter. These will also be the best places to start for anyone looking to research Syon's history further. From here, readers may want to graduate to the full scholarly bibliographies that are maintained on the website of the Syon Abbey Society (https://syonabbeysociety.wordpress.com/). For background information for each chapter I have also used a range of standard reference works, amongst which I should make special mention of the *Oxford Dictionary of National Biography* (online edition).

General sources for Syon's history

(I have drawn on these for several of my chapters, as detailed further below.)

Aungier, G. J., *The History and Antiquities of Syon Monastery, the Parish of Isleworth, and the Chapelry of Hounslow* (London: J. B. Nichols & Son, 1840).

De Hamel, Christopher, *Syon Abbey: The Library of the Bridgettine Nuns and their Peregrinations after the Reformation. An Essay by Christopher de Hamel, with the Manuscript at Arundel Castle* (London: Roxburghe Club, 1991).

Ellis, Roger, *Viderunt eam filie Syon: The Spirituality of the English House of a Medieval Contemplative Order from its Beginnings to the Present Day*, Analecta Cartusiana 68 (Salzburg: Institut für Anglistik und Amerikanistik Universität Salzburg, 1984).

Fletcher, John Rory, *The Story of the English Bridgettines of Syon Abbey* (South Brent: Syon Abbey, 1933).

Fletcher's manuscript notebooks (35 volumes): Exeter University Library 95/1–35.

Johnston, F. R., 'Syon Abbey', in *The Victoria History of the County of Middlesex. Vol. 1* (Oxford, 1961), pp. 182–91.

Jones, E. A., and Alexandra Walsham, eds, *Syon Abbey and its Books: Reading, Writing and Religion c. 1400–1700* (Woodbridge: Boydell & Brewer, 2010).

Tait, M. B., *A Fair Place: Syon Abbey 1415–1539* (CreateSpace Independent Publishing Platform, 2013).

Material on Syon's history was published in the community's own magazine, *The Poor Soul's Friend, and St Joseph's Monitor*, later known as *Syon Abbey* (1893–1974). A brief account of the magazine's foundation is given in Chapter 6.

1. Beginnings

There are accounts of the foundation in Aungier, Johnston, and Tait. Also useful (especially for the primary documents she includes) is the excursus on the founding of Syon in Margaret Deanesly, *The Incendium Amoris of Richard Rolle of Hampole* (Manchester: Manchester University Press, 1915).

For the proposed foundation in York, see Eric Graff, 'A Neglected Episode in the Prehistory of Syon Abbey: The Letter of Katillus Thornberni in Uppsala University Library Pappersbrev 1410–1420', *Mediaeval Studies* 63 (2001), 323–36. For relations with Vadstena, see Elin Andersson, 'Birgittines in Contact: Early Correspondence between England and Vadstena', *Eranos* 102 (2004), 1–29; and *Responsiones Vadstenenses: Perspectives on the Birgittine Rule in Two Texts from Vadstena and Syon Abbey* (Stockholm: Stockholms Universitet, 2011).

For Henry V as founder, see Neil Beckett, 'St. Bridget, Henry V, and Syon Abbey', in *Studies in St. Birgitta and the Birgittine Order*, ed. James Hogg (Salzburg: Institut für Anglistik und Amerikanistik Universität Salzburg, 1993), ii.125–50; and more broadly Jeremy Catto, 'Religious Change under Henry V', in *Henry V: The Practice of Kingship*, ed. G. L. Harriss (Oxford: Oxford University Press, 1985), pp. 97–115.

2. Medieval Syon

For Thomas Fishbourne and the controversy over double orders, see Hans Cnattingius, *Studies in the Order of St. Bridget of Sweden I: The Crisis in the 1420s.* (Stockholm: Almqvist och Wiksell, 1963).

A convenient modern English translation of Syon legislative material is *Rule of Our Most Holy Saviour and the Additions* (?Plymouth, 1914). This represents the early-twentieth-century reinterpretation of the rules and constitutions, however, and does not in all respects accurately reflect medieval practice. The Middle English material is gathered by James Hogg in *The Rewyll of Seynt Sauioure and other Middle English Brigittine Legislative Texts* (Salzburg: Institut für Anglistik und Amerikanistik Universität Salzburg, 1980). See further the study by Ellis, *Viderunt eam filie Syon*.

For the Syon nuns, see F. R. Johnston, 'Joan North, First Abbess of Syon, 1420–33', in *Birgittiana* 1 (1996), 47–68; and the work of Virginia Bainbridge, especially her essay 'Syon Abbey: Women and Learning *c.* 1415–1600', in *Syon Abbey and its Books*. For the brothers, see Tait; Peter Cunich, 'The Brothers of Syon, 1420–1695', in *Syon Abbey and its Books*; and a number of studies by Vincent Gillespie, most notably his *Syon Abbey*, with *The Libraries of the Carthusians*, ed. A. I. Doyle, Corpus of British Medieval Library Catalogues 9 (London: The British Library, 2001).

Evidence for building work at Syon is collected by R. W. Dunning, 'The Building of Syon Abbey', *Transactions of the Ancient Monuments Society* 25 (1981), 16–26. For the brethren's preaching, see studies by Susan Powell, including 'Preaching at Syon Abbey', *Leeds Studies in English*, n.s. 31 (2000), 229–67; and for pious friends and lodgers, Mary C. Erler, *Women, Reading and Piety in Late Medieval England* (Cambridge: Cambridge University Press, 2006), chapter 4.

3. The Road to Exile

For the humanism of the brothers and their books, see Gillespie; and for the context, Maria Dowling, *Humanism in the Age of Henry VIII* (London: Croom Helm, 1986).

For the writings and print publications of the Syon brethren see Alexandra Da Costa, *Reforming Printing: Syon Abbey's Defence of Orthodoxy 1525–1534* (Oxford: Oxford University Press, 2012).

For Syon during the dissolution see Tait, and Cunich in *Syon Abbey and its Books*. A recent study of the period that includes a substantial discussion of Syon is G. W. Bernard, *The King's Reformation: Henry*

VIII and the Remaking of the English Church (New Haven: Yale University Press, 2007).

4. Wanderings

For the aftermath of the Henrician dissolution, see Cunich in *Syon Abbey and its Books*, and his 'The Syon Household at Denham, 1539–50', in *Religion and the Household*, ed. John Doran *et al.*, Studies in Church History 50 (Woodbridge: Ecclesiastical History Society, 2014), pp. 174–87; Mary C. Erler, *Reading and Writing During the Dissolution: Monks, Friars and Nuns 1530–1558* (Cambridge: Cambridge University Press, 2013), chapters 5–6.

For the transfer of the Isleworth site to lay ownership, see G. R. Batho, *Syon House: The First Two Hundred Years, 1431–1632* (London: Middlesex Archaeological Society, 1956).

The exile in the Low Countries is described in Fletcher, and more fully in his notebooks, Exeter University Library 95/5–6; for Rouen, see Exeter University Library 95/7–9. For this period we also have narratives produced by the community itself: *The Wanderings of Syon* (published in serial form in *The Poor Soul's Friend*, though I have used the copy with manuscript annotations by Canon Fletcher in Exeter University Library 95/19), and the pictorial history of these years presented in De Hamel. See further Ann M. Hutchison, 'Transplanting the Vineyard: Syon Abbey 1539–1861', in *Der Birgittenorden in der frühen Neuzeit*, ed. Wilhelm Liebhart (Frankfurt am Main: Peter Lang, 1998), pp. 79–107.

For context, see Claire Walker, 'Continuity and Isolation: The Bridgettines of Syon in the Sixteenth and Seventeenth Centuries', in *Syon Abbey and its Books*; Paul Lee, *Learning and Spirituality in Late Medieval English Society: The Dominican Priory of Dartford* (Woodbridge: York Medieval Press, 2001).

5. Lisbon

The early years in Lisbon are described in detail in the final chapters of *The Wanderings of Syon*. Nineteenth-century copies of some early charters and other documents are in The National Archives, FO 63/268/736. Two sets of unpublished Syon annals overlap, and between them cover (albeit patchily) the rest of the time in Lisbon. The annals in Exeter University Library MS 389/1974 (formerly described as Box 28) run up to *c.* 1738 and are here referred to as the 'Lisbon Annals' (I have used a transcription very kindly provided by Caroline Bowden). The annals in Exeter University Library MS 389/3948 were written up from oral testimony and handed-down tradition after the return to England, and are here known, from the place where they were recorded, as the 'Chudleigh Annals'. For an overview see Caroline Bowden, 'Books and Reading at Syon Abbey, Lisbon, in the Seventeenth Century', in *Syon Abbey and its Books.*

For legislation, see Ellis, chapter 4; James Hogg, *Carthusian Abstinence: Birgittine Legislation for Syon Abbey Lisbon,* Analecta Cartusiana 35: 14 (Salzburg: Institut für Anglistik und Amerikanistik Universität Salzburg, 1991); materials in Box 35 of the Syon Abbey archive (Exeter University Library MS 389/2604–19).

The full title of Robinson's *Anatomy* is *The anatomy of the English nunnery at Lisbon in Portugall Dissected and laid open by one that was sometime a yonger brother of the conuent: who (if the grace of God had not preuented him) might haue growne as old in a wicked life as the oldest among them* (London: George Purslowe, 1622); Seth Foster's response has been edited by James Hogg, 'Answer to an attack on the nuns of Sion contained in a book entitled "The Anatomy of the English Nunnery at Lisbon" by Thomas Robinson, London, 1622 (signed 16 Dec 1622) from British Library Add. MSS 21203, Gf. 42b. Papers relating to English Jesuits', in *Analecta Cartusiana* 244 (2006), 85–121.

The life of Leonor de Mendanha, and Sr Catherine Witham's letter describing the earthquake, are in *English Convents in Exile, 1600–1800. Volume 3: Life Writing I,* ed. Nicky Hallett (London: Pickering & Chatto, 2012). Other nuns are listed in the online database 'Who Were the Nuns?' at http://wwtn.history.qmul.ac.uk.

The other anglophone religious houses in Lisbon have all recently found historians, whose work provides invaluable context. See Patricia O'Connell, *The Irish College at Lisbon, 1590–1834* (Dublin: Four Courts Press, 2001); Honor McCabe, *A Light Undimmed: The Convent of Our Lady of Bom Sucesso* (Dublin: Dominican Publications, 2007); Simon Johnson, *The English College at Lisbon. Volume 1: From Reformation to Toleration* (Bath: Downside Abbey Press, 2014).

6. Return

There are brief accounts of Syon's return to England in Fletcher and De Hamel; Aungier has details of the failed return led by Abbess Dorothy Halford, but he wrote before the return of 1861. The principal narrative source for the community that remained in Lisbon is the 'Chudleigh Annals'. There is excellent material on Spetisbury in Sue Stead, 'The History of St. Monica's Priory, Spetisbury, Dorset', https://sites.google.com/site/stmonicaspriory/. For Chudleigh, see http://www.chudleighhistorygroup.com/convents.html.

For the return of the exiled monastic communities more generally, see *The Great Return: The English Communities in Continental Europe and their Repatriation 1793 & 1794*, ed. Aidan Bellenger (English Benedictine Congregation History Commission, 1993; now available from http://www.plantata.org.uk); and, for the founding of new ones, Barbara Walsh, *Roman Catholic Nuns in England and Wales 1800–1937: A Social History* (Dublin: Irish Academic Press, 2002); Carmen Mangion, *Contested Identities: Catholic Women Religious in Nineteenth-Century England and Wales* (Manchester: Manchester University Press, 2008); Susan O'Brien, 'Religious Life for Women', in *From without the Flaminian Gate: 150 Years of Roman Catholicism in England and Wales 1850–2000*, ed. Alan McClelland and Michael Hodgetts (London: Darton, Longman and Todd, 1999), pp. 108–41.

I have an account of the quincentenary celebrations in 1920, based on materials from the Syon archive, in preparation. The pamphlet *Five Centuries Record of the English Bridgettines of Syon Abbey 1420–1920* (South Brent: Syon Abbey, 1920), by Dudley Baxter, was published anonymously.

Brief accounts of Adam Hamilton and John Rory Fletcher are given by Ann Hutchison, 'Syon Abbey Preserved: Some Historians of Syon', in *Syon Abbey and its Books*. The Syon archive includes a typescript draft 'Father Benedict Williamson: priest, architect, and religious founder', by Brocard Sewell, O. Carm., dated 1987, at Exeter University Library MS 389/3278.

7. The Final Century

There is no printed history covering this period. A source of useful information about the community, including professions, jubilees and deaths, but also a wide range of incidental material, is the brief section of 'Syon Notes' included in most issues of *The Poor Soul's Friend*. The chapter is, otherwise, largely based on unpublished primary materials selected from the Syon Abbey archive now at the University of Exeter. Further insights have come from conversations with Sr Anne Smyth.

For the move from Chudleigh to Marley House, see especially the materials in Box 14 (Exeter University Library MS 389/1063–1259).

For revision of the Syon legislation in light of Vatican II, see the brief appendix in Ellis, and the materials in the archive, especially Box 78 (Exeter University Library MS 389/4102–3) and a recently acquired, uncatalogued box. For the translation of the liturgy, see Sr Anne Smyth's introduction to *Daily Office of Our Lady: The Syon Breviary*, ed. Anne Smyth *et al.* (Plymouth: The Bridgettine Sisters, at press).

On the closure of the convent, see Ann M. Hutchison, 'Syon Abbey Today', in *Syon Abbey Society Newsletter* 2 (2012), https://syonabbey society.wordpress.com/newsletter/.

INDEX

The index was compiled with the assistance of Katie Ashcroft-Jones. Page references in italic type refer to illustrations.